THEN AND THERE SERIES

GENERAL EDITOR

MARJORIE REEVES

The Jacobite Rising of 1745

WILLIAM STEVENSON, M.A.

Illustrated from contemporary sources

LONGMAN

LONGMAN GROUP LIMITED
London
*Associated companies, branches and representatives
throughout the world*

© Longman Group Limited 1968

First published 1968
Ninth impression 1980

ISBN 0 582 20414 3

Printed in Hong Kong by
Dai Nippon Printing Co (H.K.) Ltd

FOR PAT AND RANDALL

ACKNOWLEDGEMENTS

For their assistance with the preparation of his book the author would like to thank
Peter B. Clarke, M.A., F.L.A., Principal Librarian, Jordanhill College of Education,
and the Library Staff there; William A. McNeill, M.A., 33 Oakfield Avenue, Glasgow
W.2; and Wilfred Norris, B.A., B.Mus., F.R.C.O., Principal Lecturer in Music,
Jordanhill College of Education.

We are also grateful to the following for permission to reproduce the following
illustrations: J. Allan Cash—page 67; Earl of Ancaster and the Scottish National
Portrait Gallery—page 80; His Grace the Duke of Atholl—pages 35, 42 and 82;
Bibliothèque Nationale, Paris—page 96; Bodleian Library, Oxford—page 97; British
Museum—pages 48, 50, 59, 64, 83, 84, 89 and 94 top; Derby Public Libraries—page 56;
The Director, Glasgow Museum and Art Galleries—page 24 (all except musket);
Gerard Holdsworth Productions Ltd. (photograph by Mr. Don Kelly)—page 95;
Manchester Public Libraries—page 53; Mansell Collection—page 47; Earl of Mar
and Kellie, and the Scottish National Portrait Gallery—page 10; Master of the
Armouries, H.M. Tower of London (Crown Copyright Reserved)—page 24 (musket
only); Mitchell Library, Glasgow—page 62; Mr. Victor Montagu—page 33; Scottish
National Portrait Gallery—pages vii, 20, 29 and 66; National Portrait Gallery—pages
1, 3, 71 and 94 bottom; National Trust for Scotland—page 73; W. A. Poucher,
F.R.P.S.—page 39; Radio Times Hulton Picture Library—pages vi, 11, 60, 72, 91 and
92; Réunion des Musées Nationaux, France—page 32; Society of Antiquaries of
Scotland—page 16; Thomas Coram Foundation for Children—page 55; Valentine &
Sons Ltd., Dundee—page 90; Captain Michael Wemyss—page 77; West Highland
Museum, Fort William—page 38. The photograph on page 86 is reproduced by
gracious permission of Her Majesty the Queen and that on page 5 is from the collection
of Dr. J. S. Richardson—on loan to the Scottish National Portrait Gallery.

CONTENTS

Page

TO THE READER

On 17 April of the year 1719 four Irish soldiers, Captain Wogan, Captain Misset, Captain O'Toole and Major Gaydon, rode out of Strasburg, a town on the banks of the River Rhine, and headed eastwards. This may not seem to be very odd or unusual, as many Irishmen were to be found in foreign armies at this time, but these men had a very romantic mission to carry out. They were to rescue a Polish princess who was imprisoned in a castle at Innsbruck in southern Austria! Captain Misset's wife accompanied them as a companion for the princess if the rescue succeeded, and a servant-girl called Jenny, who had a very important part to play in their plan as well. Captain Wogan had already visited Innsbruck disguised as a French pedlar, and the princess and her mother had agreed to his plan for the escape.

After a journey of ten days they arrived at Innsbruck in a storm of wind and rain—the very best kind of weather for their purpose—and were met by one of the princess's servants called Chateaudeau, who took Jenny with him and returned to the castle, where the princess and her mother were waiting. Jenny was very tall and the princess was short, so the former had to wear slippers instead of her high-heeled shoes. Then, when they got into the castle Jenny gave her cloak and hood to the princess, who said goodbye to her mother, took up a parcel of her jewels, and, disguised as the servant and accompanied by Chateaudeau, got safely to the gate. There, Chateaudeau said goodnight in a loud voice—loud enough to reach the ears of Captain Wogan, who was standing as close as he dared—and the princess slipped out past the *gate-porter**.

The Captain led her quickly to the inn where the others were waiting, and, stopping only long enough for the princess to change her shoes and stockings (she had stepped into several large puddles on the way!), the party set off towards the

*Words printed in italics will be found in the Glossary on page 103.

Italian border. They had gone only a few miles, however, when it was discovered that the princess's parcel of jewels had been left behind, and Captain O'Toole rode back at a gallop to the inn. Of course, he did not dare knock at the door, for it was now the middle of the night and the escape would have been discovered too soon: but, being a very strong man, he lifted the inn door off its hinges, picked up the parcel of jewels from the table and caught up with the party again.

This was far from being the end of the adventure. Jenny kept up the pretence of being the princess as long as she could by staying in bed and pretending to be ill; but, when the truth was discovered, a messenger was sent to the governor of the next large town to tell him to prevent the princess from going any farther. Luckily, Captain Misset and Captain O'Toole were coming along behind as a rearguard and met the messenger at an inn, where they treated him so hospitably that 'in a little the poor German was in such a Pickle that he was fitter to go to Bed than get a [on] Horseback!'

In the meantime, the others were also having difficulties. The food they got was almost uneatable, and they had to make tea in a can that had previously held oil! Travellers in front of them got all the best horses, and their carriage broke down twice, so that they had to go on in a vehicle that was not much better than a cart. But, four days after the rescue, they crossed the Italian border and were safe at last.

Now, first of all, you will want to know who the princess was; and then, why she had been kept a prisoner. The first part is easy to answer, but the second requires quite a long story.

The princess was Clementina Maria Sophia Sobieska, granddaughter of the famous King John Sobieski of Poland, and she was being kept in the castle at Innsbruck to prevent her marriage to the son of King James II of England and VII of Scotland. Prince James Edward had, since his father's death

Princess Clementina Sobieska. (Can you translate what is written below the picture?)

in 1701, been recognised by his supporters as the true king of Britain. He was called by them King James III of England and VIII of Scotland, but he is best remembered as the 'Old Pretender'. (The word Pretender comes from the French word 'prétendant', which means 'claimant'.) Thanks to the four Irish soldiers, James and Clementina were married soon after her rescue and their eldest son was born on the last day of December 1720. He was given the names Charles Edward Louis Philip Casimir, and, as you know, he was the leader of the 1745 Jacobite rising.

In order to understand why someone tried to prevent this

Prince James Edward Stuart, the 'Old Pretender'

marriage we must look farther back into history, to the year 1685. You will find the whole story in the Prologue and Chapter One.

Prologue

In the year 1685 King Charles II was succeeded by his brother James, but, though James lived for another sixteen years, he was king of Britain for only a little more than three. Let us see why.

Many of the Stuart rulers were very charming people, but King James II was an exception. It is true that he was a sin-

King James II and VII

cere and conscientious person, but his manner was completely different from that of his elder brother, who, you may remember, was called the 'Merry Monarch'. It was said of James that he never forgot an enemy and seldom remembered a friend; but, though he was obstinate and sometimes cruel, the trouble in his reign really began over religion. James had been converted to the Roman Catholic religion, and, when he became king, it was soon clear to everyone that he intended to restore that religion to Britain. Although it was against the law, Catholics were appointed as officers in the army, a Catholic was made Admiral of the navy, others were given important positions in the government and the universities and freedom of worship was granted to all *Nonconformists*. All this was very alarming to most people in England and Scotland; but, what was worse, James was doing these things without the consent of parliament, which he had prorogued (that is, ended its meetings for the time being) at the beginning of his reign. It seemed to many that James was trying to rule Britain in the same way as his cousin, Louis XIV, was then ruling France—that is, as an absolute monarch.

This was very serious indeed, but it is just possible that the people might have been willing to put up with James for the rest of his life, because everyone knew that the heir to the throne was his daughter Mary, who was a Protestant, and who was married to William, the ruler of Holland, who was a Protestant also. (The succession table on page 4 makes this clear.) Unfortunately for James, in June 1688, his wife had a son, who at once became the *heir-apparent*. Naturally, this boy, who would one day become the ruler of Britain instead of his half-sister Mary, would be brought up as a Catholic, and many people feared that he would be sure to follow in his father's footsteps. To prevent such a thing happening, a number of important people wrote to Holland and asked William to come to England's assistance.

King William III

The rest of the story is soon told. William gathered an army and landed at Torbay in Devonshire. As he marched towards London an ever-increasing number of supporters joined him; James sent his family to France for safety, and, when he saw that only a few people were prepared to stand by him, he followed them himself soon afterwards. Parliament then met and agreed that James had abdicated the throne; and they offered it to William and Mary, who accepted. At the same time, a number of laws were passed to prevent any future sovereign from trying to rule as James had done. That is why this is called the 'Glorious Revolution', because it ensured that parliament, which represents the people and is elected by the people, really controls the government of the country.

Though William and Mary were accepted as rulers by the Parliaments of England and Scotland, this did not mean that they were welcomed by everyone. A number of people continued to think of James as the true king of Britain, and, when he died, they accepted his son as James III of England and VIII of Scotland, as we saw on page vi. We call these people *Jacobites*, because 'Jacobus' is the Latin word for James. They tried several times to alter what had happened in 1689 and to place James on the throne, and in Chapter One we shall find out something about these earlier risings before we begin our study of the 1745 rebellion.

SUCCESSION TABLE

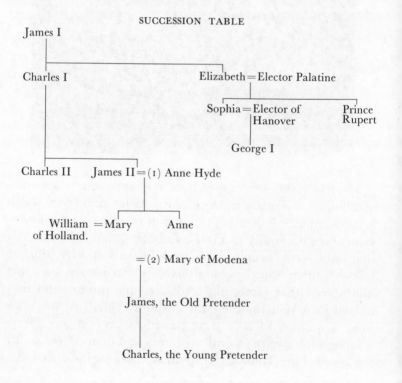

1　The Early Jacobite Risings

The first Jacobite rising took place in Scotland in the same
year as the 'Glorious Revolution', and we can read how it
began in the first verse of Sir Walter Scott's song, 'Bonnie
Dundee'.

To the Lords of Convention 'twas Claver'se who spoke,
　'Ere the King's crown shall fall there are crowns to be
　　broke;
　So let each Cavalier who loves honour and me,
　Come follow the bonnet of Bonnie Dundee.'

By the Lords of Convention Sir Walter meant the parliament
which met in Scotland soon after James's flight; and you will
remember that the King's supporters in the Civil War were
called 'Cavaliers'. The 'Bonnie Dundee' of the song was John
Graham of Claverhouse, Viscount Dundee, who had played a

Viscount Dundee

5

big part in hunting down the *Covenanters* in the reigns of Charles II and his brother. He now raised some of the High- land clans to fight for James and end the Revolution—that is what is meant by the words '. . . there are crowns to be broke'.

In July 1689 Major-General Mackay was sent to deal with this rising. He met Dundee's army just beyond the pass of Killiecrankie in Perthshire, but the Highlanders took a posi- tion higher up the slope than the government troops and attacked them suddenly just before sunset. Their advance was so rapid that Mackay's men could fire only once, and had no time to fix bayonets before their ranks were broken by the charging clansmen: but it was a costly victory for the rebels, since Dundee was mortally wounded as he was waving his men on to the pursuit. His followers then tried to capture Dunkeld, but were driven off by a troop of Covenanters, and they were finally routed at Cromdale on Speyside. This ended the only Scottish attempt to restore James II to his throne, but, when he died, his son James was recognised as king by the Jacobites, as we have seen. We will look now at their early attempts to put him on the throne.

1708

The first attempt was made when James's half-sister Anne was Queen. The parliaments of the two countries had been united in 1707, and later on this union brought many benefits to Scotland, but in 1708 many Scots thought that they had made a bad bargain, so it was likely that they would welcome James. Also, Britain was then fighting France in the War of the Spanish Succession, and there were only about 1,500 govern- ment troops in the whole of Scotland, so you can see that this was a good time for the Jacobites to try to win the throne for James. Louis XIV of France gave him ships and about 5,000 men to help him in his landing, but somehow everything seemed to go wrong. Here is how the French commander of the expedition described what happened:

'The King of England arrived [at Dunkirk]. . . . Whether from fatigue or some other cause, the King fell ill of measles, and for two days was in a fever. The delay which his illness caused allowed the enemy time to *reconnoitre* our position. Thirty-eight English Men-of-War anchored off Gravelines, two leagues from Dunkirk. . . .

. . . The wind becoming favourable, we set sail, and on the third day were off the Coast of Scotland, in sight of Land. Our Pilots had made an error of six leagues in their bearings. They altered our course, and the Wind and Tide becoming contrary, we anchored at night-fall at the mouth of the Edinburgh River [the Firth of Forth]. . . .

In vain we made Signals, lit Fires and fired our Cannon; nobody appeared . . . At daybreak we discovered the English Fleet anchored at four leagues distance from us. The sight of them caused me considerable uneasiness. We were shut in a sort of Bay, with a Cape to be *doubled* before we could gain the open sea.'

The French commander succeeded in escaping from this trap, but he refused to take the risk of allowing James to land anywhere else on the coast and the expedition returned to France. Here is a Jacobite description of the effect of the news of James's arrival and departure on the people of Edinburgh:

'Never was seen so universal a joy as that which appeared in everybody's countenance. . . . The loyal subjects thronged together and those of the government *durst* not appear in public. They had no confidence in the regular troops, knowing that the best part, both of the officers and the soldiers, were *well-affected* to the king [that is, James]. Besides, there was neither powder nor ammunition in the castle of Edinburgh, nor in that of Stirling; and they knew that all the gentry would revolt from the government the moment the king landed. . . . But no sooner was it known by the *gazettes* that the king was returned to Dunkirk, than the consternation was so-great, that everybody appeared distracted.'

Thus, through no fault of his own, James lost what was perhaps the best chance he ever had of gaining the British crown.

1715

Seven years later the Jacobites tried again, and, with better leadership, this rebellion could have been a much more serious affair than it was.

Queen Anne died in 1714 and was succeeded by George, the *Elector* of Hanover. (You can see why a German ruler became king of Britain by looking at the table on page 4.) This would have been the right moment to start a rebellion—can you think why?—but no real plans had been made to do so, and the chance was lost. A Scottish minister wrote this comment:

'Agust, 1714. This moneth makes a vast change by the Queen's death, and the peacable proclamation of King George. The joy soe great and universall, that I have seen nothing like it since the Revolution, when I was but young. This is a wonderful *dash* to the Jacobites; and had the Queen lived a little longer, they think their schemes would have taken effect. . . . Houever, "the Lord hath broken the snare, and we are escaped".'

(You can guess for yourself which side the writer of this belonged to.)

But even a year later, in 1715, the rebellion still had some chance of success, for George was not popular in either Scotland or England, as we can tell from the words of this song:

Old H[anover] does Turnips sell
    And through the streets does cry them;
Young Noodle leads about the Ass
    To such as please to buy them;

8

Such Folks as these can never be
   Compar'd to Royal J-m-y,
Who is our true and lawfull King;
   I hope ere long he'll see me.

(It was a favourite joke at this time to pretend that, because turnips were introduced into England from Hanover, they were almost the only food of the royal family! Can you guess why 'Hanover' and 'Jamey' were not spelled out in full, and who 'Young Noodle' was?)

The 1715 rebellion was something of a muddle from the very beginning. The government knew about the plans that the Jacobites were making and the navy watched the French ports carefully. Attempts made by the Duke of Ormonde to land on the south coast of England failed from lack of support; and the rising was finally started in Scotland by the Earl of Mar without James's permission!

John Erskine, the Earl of Mar, was about the worst person for a commander-in-chief that could be imagined. Though he had been a Secretary of State for Scotland and had helped to get the Treaty of Union passed in 1707, it is believed that his nickname 'Bobbing John' was given him because he could not be relied upon. George I knew this, and when Mar attended the new King's *levée* on 1 August 1715, George deliberately ignored him. The next day Mar left London in a coal boat, landed at Elie in Fife and went north to Braemar, where he began to assemble James's supporters.

One of those who played a big part in the rebellion was a man with the same Christian names as the Old Pretender, James Francis Edward Keith, who, many years later, became a famous soldier, first in Russia and then in Prussia, where Frederick the Great made him a Field Marshal. Here is what he wrote about the beginning of the rising:

'The Earl of Mar, under pretence of a great hunting, had already assembled about 800 men, and with these he set

9

The Earl of Mar

up the Royal standard, proclaimed King James, King of
Scotland, England, France and Ireland, and published a
declaration in which he *deduced* all the misfortunes the
Revolution had brought on the Kingdome of Scotland,
and particularly the hardships it groan'd under since the
fatal union, and concluded that he had taken arms by the
orders of their lawfull Souveraign, to free them from a
burthen they were no longer able to bear. . . . Every thing
being now ready for beginning the enterprize, the Earl of
Marr order'd the Highland chiefs of the clans to assemble
their men with all possible hast. . . . In the midst of these

preparations arrived the unlucky news of the King of France's death, which mightily discouraged many of our party, the *succours* we expected from him being one of the principal motives which made us *engage in the attempt.* . . . In the meantime, our troops advanced from all parts of the North of Scotland towards Perth and by the beginning of October we had assembled about five thousand foot and twelve hundred horse.'

While this was going on in the north, a plan was made which, if it had been successful, might have won Scotland for the Jacobites. This was an attempt to capture Edinburgh Castle, which at this time contained nearly all the arms and ammunition which the government had in Scotland, as well as a large sum of money. You can see that the arms, the money and the possession of the Castle would have been a great help to Mar if they could have been captured. Though the Governor of the Castle was warned that the attempt was going to be

Edinburgh Castle

made he did not take many precautions, but the plotters themselves spoiled their chances by wasting two hours in drinking to their success in a near-by tavern! When they finally reached the Castle their helpers inside the walls were discovered just as they were preparing to pull up the ladders, and so the plan failed.

The task of crushing the rising was given to the Duke of Argyll, who had served with the famous Duke of Marlborough in the War of the Spanish Succession. As soon as possible he took up his position at Stirling, and if you look at the map on page 13 you can perhaps see why this place was chosen for the government army. Since he had less than 2,000 men at this time he could not attack the Jacobite force: instead, he waited as patiently as he could, knowing that they would be sure to start marching southwards quite soon.

About a week after Mar arrived at Perth another rising began in southern Scotland, led by Viscount Kenmure, and one in northern England, led by the Earl of Derwentwater and Mr Forster, the M.P. for Northumberland. Finding little support in Scotland, Kenmure joined the other Jacobites in England, and the Earl of Mar sent about 2,500 men to help them. This force was under the command of Brigadier William Mackintosh, who, knowing that there were three men-o'-war in the Firth of Forth, sent 500 of his men openly to Burntisland to attract their attention, and then marched the remaining 2,000 secretly farther east, where they crossed the Firth in a fleet of small boats. He nearly succeeded in capturing Edinburgh, but when Argyll advanced with some of his men he gave up the attempt; and the three groups, under Kenmure, Derwentwater and Mackintosh, all met at Kelso and began to march south. (You can follow their movements on the map on page 13.)

At last, after collecting as many troops as he could from the Highlands, Mar advanced towards Stirling. Since he had

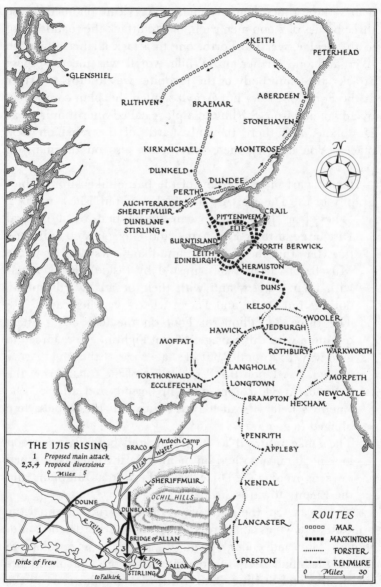

Map of the 1715 Rising

1 3

nearly three times as many men as Argyll he planned to use three bodies of 1,000 men each, one to attack the road leading to the bridge over the Forth, one to attack farther down the river and one farther up. While Argyll was meeting these attacks, the main body of the Jacobites was to cross the river at the Fords of Frew; but Argyll spoiled this plan completely by advancing from Stirling to a place called Sheriffmuir, near Dunblane, and there the only battle of the rebellion took place. (You can see these movements also on the map on page 13.)

Here is part of an account of the battle taken from a biography of the Duke of Argyll which was published in 1745:

'They [the Jacobites] began the Action by a general Discharge of their Fire Arms, and Glengarry so animated the Men, that they followed him like Furies close up to the Muzells of the Muskets, push'd by (aside) the Bayonets with their *Targets*, and with their broad Swords spread nothing but Death and Terror where-ever they came.

The three Battallions of Foot on the left, being unacquainted with this Savage Way of Fighting, were forced to give way, so a total Rout of that Wing of the royal Army ensued. . . . Upon the Right Wing of the royal Army the Duke of Argyle commanded in Person, and attack'd the Enemy's Left with such Intrepidity that the Rebels were obliged to give way. . . .

The Duke return'd to the Field, and both Parties stood looking at one another, but neither caring to engage; when towards evening the Duke drew off towards Dumblain, and the Enemy towards Ardoch.'

As you can see, the right wings of each army defeated the opposite left wings and drove them off the battlefield; and, though Mar had enough men left, he made no attempt to attack the small body of government troops that stood between him and Stirling. The words of a popular song of the time tell the story very well:

> There's some say that we wan [won],
> > Some say that they wan,
> Some say that nane wan at a', man;
> > But one thing I'm sure
> > That at Sheriffmuir
> A battle was there which I saw, man.
> And we ran and they ran, and they ran and we ran,
> > And we ran and they ran awa', man.

Oddly enough, on the very same day, 13 November, the Jacobite forces that had marched into England were trapped at Preston and had to surrender, so this was really the end of the rebellion. We will let Marshal Keith finish the story:

'News was brought us that the same day we fought the Duke of Argile's army, our troops in England had surrendered. . . . This gave the enemy opportunity to draw down forces from England against us . . . and several of our party, seeing that the English [Jacobites] were quelled . . . began to think of *making terms* for themselves.

The King arrived safely in the end of December 1715, after a great many dangers, but came in a very small fishing *barck* with only two servants, and without any of those things which we had so much depended on, so that what shou'd have given our affairs the greatest life was rather a discouragement to them.'

James saw that the game was up and sailed back to France in February 1716, taking Mar with him; and the Jacobite army, deserted by its leaders, disappeared among the hills before Argyll's forces could overtake them.

Though six of the leaders of the rebellion had been taken prisoner, four succeeded in escaping, and only Derwentwater and Kenmure were executed. The lands of those who took part were forfeited—that is, given up to the government—but no one could be found to buy them, and finally the government made a profit on them of only £1,107! A Disarming Act was passed and a great many weapons were handed in, but, when they were examined, they were found to be old and useless— the good ones were carefully hidden away. Finally, the most important result of the rising was that General Wade was sent

General Wade

to the Highlands, where, between 1725 and 1737, with the help of 500 soldiers, he built about 250 miles of roads and about forty bridges, so that all the main posts in that area were connected up for the first time with roads on which regular troops could march quickly to crush any future rebellion.

1719

Four years later the last of these early Jacobite attempts was made, this time with help from Spain. Once again the Duke of Ormonde was to land in England and a smaller force was to come to Scotland; but once again the Duke failed, this time due to stormy weather which scattered his ships. Only two Spanish ships arrived on the Scottish coast, the 300 troops which they contained were supported by only a few Highlanders and the combined force was defeated at the battle of Glenshiel.

Now you can see why the attempt was made to prevent the marriage of Prince James and Princess Clementina in 1719, that you read about at the beginning of the book. George I had asked the *Holy Roman Emperor* to keep the Princess prisoner because, if James was prevented from getting married, then he would have no heir and George's throne would not be in danger.

The Causes of Failure

We have already seen that the rebellion of 1708 failed because of bad luck as much as anything; that the 1715 was badly planned and badly led; and that the 1719 was too small to have any real chance of success. What other causes of failure were there?

In December 1714 a French agent wrote a letter saying that, though many people had known of the plans to welcome the Old Pretender to Scotland that year, no one had told the secret. He added these words:

'Si je fais jamais un complot, ce sera avec les Ecossais.'

(If I ever make a plot, it will be with the Scots.)

Actually, the French agent was wrong, for one important reason for the failure of the 1715 rebellion was that too many people knew about the Jacobites' plans. The British ambassador in Paris was able, by means of spies, to find out a great deal of what was going on at James's court at Commercy in Lorraine. The Jacobites tried to prevent this by writing their letters in simple codes, and there is an example of one printed below, written in 1715 by the Duke of Berwick to the Old Pretender. It has been turned into present-day English to make it easier to follow, and the real meanings of the coded words are inside the brackets:

'A courier has been sent to Spain to ask M. Agencour (money) from M. Rose's grandson (Philip V, king of Spain) ... Belley (Berwick, the writer himself) also asked that some *baubles* for M. Alexandre (arms for the army) might also be sent from there. . . . Varennes (ships) are getting ready to accompany M. Raucourt (James) when he begins his journey. . . . I don't like M. Rethel's (Louis XIV's) state of health, so I have advised Orbec (the Duke of Ormonde) to try to gain the goodwill of Osmond (the Duke of Orleans) . . .'

The last sentence of this letter also gives us another clue to the failure of the 1715 rising: lack of French aid. Louis XIV, who would certainly have helped the Old Pretender, died a few days before the rebellion started, and the Duke of Orleans, who was regent for the young Louis XV, did not want any trouble with Britain while the French king was still a boy. Though there were a number of ships in various French ports loaded with men and arms to help the rebellion, only one, it is believed, ever reached Scotland.

The main cause of the failure was, however, quite a simple one—few people really wanted the return of the Stuart kings. Nearly everyone believed that James would be sure to try to restore the Roman Catholic religion, so, of course, the ministers of the Church of Scotland were very much against the Old Pretender, and they had a great deal of influence over their congregations. It is true that the Earl of Mar raised over 12,000 men, but these came mainly from the Highlands, and many of them were forced to turn out by the threats of their chiefs. You remember that only a few people in southern Scotland and northern England supported the rising; and, though the Jacobites got more support in Scotland than in England, this was really due to a dislike of the Union rather than to a liking for James.

We have seen that James's best chance was probably in 1708. Twenty years later a Jacobite wrote this:

'And thus whilst no party is acting for his interest, no projects formed, nothing done to keep up the spirits of the people, the old race [that is, James's supporters] drops off by degrees and a new one sprouts up, who, knowing little more of him than what the public news papers bear, enter on the stage with coolness towards him and his cause, which consequently must daylie *languish* and in course of time be tottaly forgot. . . .'

We shall see in the following pages that he was right.

2 The Highlands

Since most of the Prince's supporters came from the Highlands of Scotland, we ought to find out what kind of people the Highlanders were, and what kind of life they led; and we can do this best by looking at descriptions of them written at or near the time of the '45.

'A Highland Clan is a set of men all bearing the same sirname, and believing themselves to be related the one to the other, and to be descended from the same common Stock. . . . all agree in *owing allegiance* to the Supreme Chief of the Clan and look upon it to be their duty to support him at all adventures.'

This was written by a man called Duncan Forbes, who was

Lord President Forbes

then *Lord President of the Court of Session* and who played quite a big part in the Rising. (Can you guess which side he supported?) He was born near Inverness and he knew a great deal about the Highlands: but, though he says that the members of a clan all had the same surname, we can tell that this was not always the case, nor were they all descended from the same person either. In fact, a clan was often really a group of people, possibly with a few different surnames, who accepted one man as their chief.

> 'The chief exercises an *arbitrary* power over his vassals, determines all differences and disputes that happen among them and *levies* taxes upon extraordinary occasions, such as the marriage of a daughter. If any one should refuse to contribute to the best of his ability, he is sure of severe treatment. . . . He [the chief] is their leader in clan quarrels, and [must] maintain such, who, by accident, are fallen to *total decay*. . . . The unlimited love and obedience of the Highlanders to their chiefs are not confined to the lower order of their followers, but are the same with those who are near them in rank.'

The writer of this was Captain Edward Burt, one of General Wade's assistants in his task of building roads through the Highlands, whose letters to a friend in London give us a good picture of this part of the country about 1730. Here is what he says about the Highlanders themselves:

> 'How often have I heard them described in London as almost giants in size! and certainly there are a great many tall men of them in and about that city. . . . The *stature* of the better sort is much the same with the English, or Low-country Scots, but the common people are generally small. . . . The Highland dress consists of a bonnet made of thrum (coarse yarn) without a brim, a short coat, a waist-coat, longer by five or six inches, short stockings or brogues. . . . Few besides gentlemen wear the trowze—that is,

A Highlander with his weapons

the breeches and stockings all of one piece and drawn on together; over this habit they wear the plaid, which is usually three yards long and two breadths wide, and the whole garb is made of chequered tartan or plaiding.... This, with the sword and pistol is chiefly their mode of dressing when in the Lowlands. ...

The common habit of the ordinary Highlander is a small part of the plaid set in folds and *girt* round the waist, and the rest is brought over the shoulders and then fastened before [in front] below the neck.'

Captain Burt is here describing the two main fashions of dress in the Highlands, the trews and the belted plaid. As he says, the lower part of the plaid was wrapped round the waist as a kilt, and the upper part could be used to cover the wearer's shoulders like a cloak; but, about this time the 'feile beag' (little kilt) was also becoming popular. This was the kilt worn as it is today. Some people believe that it was introduced by the English manager of the iron works at Glengarry, so that his workers could have more freedom of movement than they could with the belted plaid. We must remember that the tartans worn at that time were probably very unlike the so-called 'clan tartans' of today; nor was it likely that every separate clan had a different tartan of its own which only members of that clan wore, though possibly the people of one district might all wear a similar pattern.

The Highlanders have always been known as good fighters, and, though we have seen that they were not always very tall, most of them must have been very wiry and strong, and well used to hardships of all kinds. Here is a description of their method of fighting, written by the Chevalier Johnstone, who was the Prince's aide-de-camp, and who was later a soldier in the French army also:

'They advance with great rapidity, discharge their pieces when within musket-length of the enemy, and then throwing them down, draw their swords, and holding a dirk in their left hand with the target, they dart with fury on the enemy, through the smoke of their fire. When within reach of the enemy's bayonets, bending their left knee, they cover their bodies with their targets, that receive the thrusts of the bayonets, while at the same time they raise their sword arms and strike their adversary. . . . Their attack is so terrible that the best troops in Europe would with difficulty sustain it; and if the swords of the Highlanders once come in contact with them, their defeat is inevitable.'

At the time of the Rising the Highlanders lived by hunting and fishing, by raising herds of sheep and cattle and by cultivating the soil. The land was divided up in different ways in different parts of the country, but generally a part was kept by the chief for his own use, and the remainder was rented out to 'tacksmen' (men who had a lease of a piece of land), who were sometimes relatives of the chief. They were the fighting men of the clan, and they usually sublet most of their land to other tenants. Crops of oats and barley were grown, large herds of cattle and sheep were raised, and thousands of animals were driven each year from the Highlands to the cattle fairs or 'trysts' at Crieff and Falkirk. From there, large numbers went on to England, and English farmers also came north to the fairs

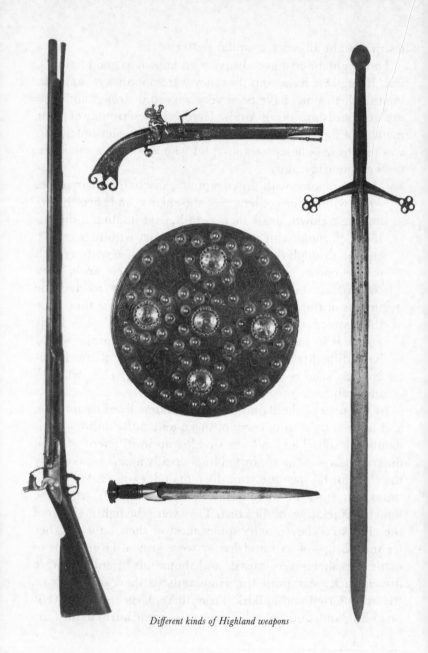

Different kinds of Highland weapons

to buy cattle for themselves.

The houses of the people were very primitive, with turf or stone walls and a thatched or turf roof, and Captain Burt says:

'When the Hut has been Built for some Time it is covered with Weeds and Grass; and, I do assure you, I have seen Sheep, that had got up from the Foot of an adjoining Hill feeding upon the Top of the House.'

The population of the Highlands at this time was possibly between 250,000 and 300,000 people, but there were large areas which had very few inhabitants. Since many people must have lived a long way from towns and burghs, the visit of the packman must have been looked forward to eagerly. These men carried their goods from house to house and village to village— plates and dishes, ribbons and beads, pins, needles and dye-stuffs for cloth—everything that people living in remote places might want. Fairs and markets were held in the burghs, and towns like Inverness would have one or two shops of different kinds. Luckily, we still have the letters of Bailie John Steuart, one of the Inverness merchants, and from these we can get a good idea of what was bought and sold at this time.

The Bailie bought large quantities of oatmeal on the east coast of Scotland and had it carried round to the west, where it was sold to the Highland chiefs and to the soldiers of the garrisons of Fort William, Glenelg and other places. He also bought salmon and other fish from the Earl of Moray and Lord Lovat, packed them in salt and exported them to all the big ports in Europe—Le Havre, Amsterdam, Bordeaux, Danzig, Stockholm, Hamburg and many others. Here is a list of some of the things that he got in return from Leghorn in Italy in 1726. They are written just as Bailie Steuart spelled them, but the difficult ones have got explanations in brackets to help you to understand what they are:

100 pd. Coffee beens	£38
2 pd. Ruburbe [used for a medicine]	£12

B

5 pd. Hypococoano [Ipecacuanha— another medicine]	£2½
50 pd. Cotton wool	£4¾
25 pd. Candied citron [sugared lemon]	£7
200 pd. Anise of Malta [plant seeds for making a drink]	£6
100 pd. Almons	£4
20 pd. prime sorte cotton yearn [yarn]	£5
20 Chest Lucca oil [used for cooking]	£4

In addition, the Bailie got barrel staves, timber, rope, iron, glass, copper and soap from the ports of the Baltic Sea; writing paper, flints and prunes from St. Martins in France; linseed oil, *madder,* azure, white lead, *verdigris,* indigo, cloves, nutmeg, tea, sugar and salt from Rotterdam; and wines of all kinds from France and Germany. He also got many little articles for his own house—warming pans and kettles, pewter dishes, *branders,* iron pots and lanterns—and he sent to London for fruit trees, yew, laurels, and variegated holly for his garden. He also sent to London for cloth for his own suits and for dresses for his wife and daughters, as we can see from this letter that he wrote in 1722:

'Please by [buy] for my use, 26 yeards striped silk, green and whyte, and 26 yeards ditto blew and wheat. It is for tuo suits of Cloaths for tuo young lasses and the price is from 3.s to 3.6d pr. yeard.'

Of course, most of the things which the Bailie and the other merchants imported would be bought only by the nobles and chiefs and the better-off tacksmen, for the ordinary Highlander would not be able to afford any luxuries such as coffee or candied citron; but these letters help us to see that life in the Highlands was not altogether as uncivilized as many people then believed it to be.

Last of all, we must remember not to fall into the trap of thinking that all Scotsmen, or even all the Highlanders, supported Prince Charlie when he landed in 1745. We are not certain just how many did so, as different writers give different numbers, but it was probably about eight or nine thousand at the most. On the other hand, three Scottish regiments fought in Cumberland's army at Culloden, and, though the Scottish nobles were not allowed to form regiments themselves, it has been calculated that between twelve and thirteen thousand Scots, mainly from the Lowlands, were ready to fight against the Prince if necessary. Even among the Highland clans, several did not take part in the Rising, or else helped the government side, like the Campbells; and so it is easy to see that, in spite of the enthusiasm of the Prince and his followers, they had really very little chance of success.

3   The Start of the Rebellion

The Young Prince

So far we have learned very little about Prince Charles Edward himself, and, since he is really the hero of this story, we shall see what can be discovered about his life before 1745.

We already know that he was born on 31 December 1720. Three years later, a writer said that 'the Prince is the first [finest] child in the world, healthy and strong, and runs about from morning to night'. In 1724 he was described as:

> 'a great musician and plays on his violin continually: no porter's child in the country has stronger legs and arms, and he makes good use of them, for he is continually in motion. . . . You may easily imagine what amusement he gives to his Father and Mother.'

When the Prince was six and a half his cousin wrote:

> 'Not only could he read fluently . . . he could ride, fire a gun, and, more surprising still, I have seen him take a cross-bow and split a rolling ball ten times in succession. He speaks English, French and Italian perfectly and altogether is the most ideal Prince I have ever met in the course of my life.'

A few years later even the chief spy of the British government admitted that Charles and his younger brother Henry attracted great attention from the English travellers in Rome, and that the elder boy was full of life and likely to be much more popular than his father.

These descriptions sound too wonderful to be true, don't they? Probably some of them were rather exaggerated, for they were written by friends or relatives: and, when Charles was thirteen, we find his tutor writing: 'The Prince grows tall and strong but it is impossible to get him to apply to any study as he ought to do, which means the Latin *goes ill,* but he

Prince Charles Edward Stuart

speaks both French and Italian easily.' Even his father admitted that 'he is mighty thoughtless and takes nothing much to heart'. From the time when he was two years old his mother and father did not get on well together—as one of the little Jacobite court said: 'Their tempers are so very different that, tho' in the greatest trifles they are never of the same opinion, the one won't yield one Inch to the other.' When Charles was almost five the Queen left the court and entered a convent, where she remained for two years, and the unhappiness which this caused may have been one reason for Charles's obstinacy and childishness in later life when things did not go as he wished.

In 1734 the Prince went off on what must have seemed to him to be a great adventure, when he accompanied his cousin, the Duke of Berwick, to the siege of the Italian town of Gaeta. He was also accompanied by his tutor, who wrote a

long letter to James describing how well the Prince had be-
haved, how eager he was to get close enough to see the fighting
and how they had visited an outpost where five cannon balls
had fallen shortly before.

> 'The Prince would have gone further if he had been
> allowed . . . . He talks to the Spanish soldiers in Spanish, to
> the *Walloons* in French, serves them with drink with his own
> hand and they can talk of nothing else. He contrasts most
> favourably with the King of Naples.'

We can see from this that the Prince was brave and that the
soldiers liked him. He had many of the qualities which make a
good leader; but, to be a successful general, one needs much
more experience than he had gained in this brief visit to a siege
when he was still only thirteen years old.

The Jacobite Attempt of 1744

In the year 1740 a young woman of twenty-three, daughter of
the Emperor Charles VI, became ruler of the lands of
Austria: and, because he thought that a girl would not be able
to defend her country as well as a man, her neighbour,
Frederick the Great of Prussia, seized a piece of Austria called
Silesia. As a result, the War of the Austrian Succession broke
out, in which Britain helped Austria and France sided with
Prussia. Oddly enough, war was not declared between Britain
and France until March 1744. Of course, the Jacobites hoped
that this war would give them a chance to put James on the
throne (can you think why?), and Prince Charles left Rome
secretly in January and arrived in Paris a month later. This
seems a long time for such a journey, but travel was slow in
these days, and the Prince wrote to his father that he had given
his companions very little rest: 'and if I had been to go much
farther I should have been obliged to get them ty'd behind the
chase with my *Portmantle* for they were quite 'rendu' [exhausted].'

In order to distract Britain's attention from the war in

Europe, the French planned to help the Jacobites to make a landing on the coast of England, so Charles went on to Gravelines, near Dunkirk, where an expedition was being made ready under the command of the famous soldier Count Maurice of Saxe. By 3 March everything was prepared, and Admiral Roqueville with a fleet of twenty ships appeared off Dungeness ready to help Count Maurice's transports to cross the Channel. As you can imagine, there was a good deal of alarm in England. The author Horace Walpole wrote in January: 'all is distraction. . . . How will it end? No joy but in the Jacobites.' And in February he said: 'As yet there is no rising, but we must expect it at the first descent [French landing]. . . . All is at stake: we have great hopes, but they are but hopes.' Prince Charlie, too, was very hopeful: 'I have the most encouraging accounts possible from the King's friends in England. . . . They are certain of my meeting with no resistance.'

Alas for the Prince's hopes! A gale from the east suddenly blew up, the French squadron was driven from its position, and many of the troop transports went aground or were severely damaged. The attempt was a complete failure; but, even if there had been no storm, it is not very likely that it would have succeeded. Admiral Norris was in the Channel and his ships could have done great damage to the expedition as it sailed across; and, though the Prince's friends were sure that there would be no resistance when he landed, do you think that this is likely if he had appeared with an army supplied by Britain's enemy?

Charles was bitterly disappointed, but he hoped that the King of France would help him again, so he took a little house in Montmartre, near Paris, where he lived till the end of 1744. We can get a good picture of the life he led from this letter to his father, which is printed just as he wrote it. You will notice that Charles does not spell very well!

Louis XV, King of France

'. . . nobody nose where I am and what is become of me, so that I am entirely Burried as to the publick and cant but say that it is a very great *constrent* upon me for I am obliged very often not to stur out of my room for fier of some bodys noing my face. I very often think that you would laugh very hartily if you saw me goin about with a single servant bying fish and other things and squabling for a peney more or less.'

The Prince waited for nearly a year to see if Louis XV would help him again, but, as time passed, he began to lose patience, both with the French and with the Jacobites in England. 'The truth of the matter is that our friends in England are affred of their own shaddo,' he wrote, 'and think of little else but diverting themselves; otherwise we would not want the King of France.' Then, in May 1745 came better news—Count Maurice of Saxe had defeated George II's son the Duke of Cumberland at the battle of Fontenoy. James was hopeful that the French would think this a good opportunity to help the Prince again; but he did not know that Charles had grown tired of waiting and had decided to take matters into his own hands. Some of the Scottish Jacobites had already asked him to land in their country with a French force; but, when it seemed that the French were not going to help him again, he made up his mind to go to Scotland alone!

His first problem was money, and, by getting his father to *pawn* some of the jewels he had left behind and by borrowing from bankers in Paris he raised enough to buy 1,500 muskets, 1,800 broadswords, 20 small guns (two of which could be carried by a mule), ammunition and *flints* for the muskets as well as other necessary supplies. He also managed to get two ships, the 'Elizabeth' and the 'Du Teillay', and on 5 July 1745 he sailed from St Nazaire at the mouth of the River Loire, accompanied by only seven companions. Almost at once the two ships ran into trouble, for they were attacked by the

The fight between the 'Lion' and the 'Elizabeth'

33

British man-o'-war 'Lion', and she and the 'Elizabeth' fought together for nearly five hours. When the battle ended the 'Elizabeth' had lost nearly 300 men killed or wounded, and was so badly damaged that she had to return to France, carrying all the arms and ammunition. The captain of the Prince's ship had wisely refused to take part in the fighting in case the Prince's life was endangered; but, in spite of this serious loss, the 'Du Teillay' sailed on alone for Scotland. On 23 July the Prince landed on the little island of Eriskay in the Outer Hebrides, and the great adventure had begun!

Note on dates

The calendar which we have today came into use only seven years after the '45, that is, in 1752. In that year eleven days were taken out of the month of September in order to correct an error in the old method of measuring time, so that the day after 2 September was not 3 September but 14 September. At the same time, the first day of the year was made 1 January, as it is now, and not 25 March, as it had been before—though the latter change had been made in Scotland in 1600. The dates which you see in these pages are the dates as they were in Prince Charlie's day, and we call them 'Old Style'.

The Raising of the Standard

Before we start on our way south with the Prince, let us look for a moment at the men who had come with him from France, especially the ones that we will be meeting from time to time later in the story. They were called the 'Seven Men of Moidart' after the area of the mainland where the party finally landed.

First, there were two Scotsmen. One was Aeneas Mac-Donald, a banker in Paris, who, it was hoped, would persuade some of his relatives living in this part of the Highlands to join the Prince; and the other was William, Marquis of Tullibardine. The latter was very nearly sixty years of age and had already taken part in the rebellions of 1715 and 1719. As a result, he had been found guilty of *high treason*, so that his younger brother James became the Duke of Atholl when their father died, instead of William. The Jacobites called them 'Duke James' and 'Duke William', but looked on William as the real Duke.

'Duke William'

Then there were four Irishmen. They were Sir Thomas Sheridan, who was over seventy and much too old for all the marching and fighting that had to be done; George Kelly, a parson, who knew nothing about war and who was distrusted by King James; Sir John MacDonald, who was probably nearly sixty, but who had had some experience of warfare in the French army; and John William O'Sullivan. The latter was the only one of the party who had any real military experience, as he, too, had fought with the French in Corsica and Italy; so, when the army was formed, he was made *Adjutant* and *Quarter-master General* to the Forces. Unluckily, as we shall see, he and the Prince's General, Lord George Murray, disliked one another intensely and could never agree about anything.

Finally, there was one Englishman, Francis Strickland, but he died at Carlisle just before it was captured by government troops. It was not a very impressive group that Charles had chosen for his companions, was it? What kind of people would you have taken with you on this adventure if you had been in the Prince's place?

Charles's memories of their first landing on the island of Eriskay could not have been happy ones. First, there was no food to be had, so the party had to catch some flounders and roast them over a small fire to make a meal. It became very wet and stormy, but when they got shelter in a house the Prince found it almost impossible to stay indoors. As in most houses of this type the fire was in the middle of the floor and a hole in the roof served as a chimney, but the smoke escaped so slowly that the room was constantly full of it, and the Prince was almost choked! The next day was no better, for the head of one of the branches of the MacDonald clan arrived and warned Charles that he could not rely on some of the chiefs that he had hoped would support him. He also advised him to return home, but the Prince replied: 'I am come home, sir, and I will *entertain no notion* of returning, for I am *persuaded* that my faithful Highlanders will stand by me.'

Leaving Eriskay, the little expedition sailed over to the mainland, where they landed at a place called Borrodale. (You can see these places on the map on the endpapers.) Messages were sent to people that the Prince thought would help him; but, as we can see from the following report, his arrival caused both alarm and amazement:

'Mr Hugh MacDonald happened to meet MacDonald of Kenlochmoydart, who asked him, "What news?" "No news at all have I," said Mr Hugh. "Then," said Kenlochmoydart, "I'll give you news. You'll see the Prince this night." "What Prince do you mean?" said Mr Hugh. "Prince Charles," said Kenlochmoydart. "You are certainly joking," said Mr Hugh, "I cannot believe you." Upon this Kenlochmoydart assured him of the truth of it. "Then," said Mr Hugh, "what number of men has he brought along with him?" "Only seven," said Kenlochmoydart. "What stock of money and arms has he brought with him then?" said Mr Hugh. "A very small stock of either," said Kenlochmoydart. "What generals or officers fitt for commanding are with him?" said Mr Hugh. "None at all," replied Kenlochmoydart. Mr Hugh said he did not like the expedition at all, and was afraid of the consequences. "I cannot help it," said Kenlochmoydart. "If the matter go wrong, then I'll certainly be hanged, for I am engaged [in it] already." '

MacDonald of Kinlochmoidart was the first to promise to support the Prince, but other MacDonald leaders—Glengarry, Keppoch and Glencoe—urged him to give up and return to France, as a rebellion without French help could not succeed. It must have been a bad moment for the Prince, but, turning from MacDonald of Clanranald to young Ranald MacDonald, a brother of his first supporter, he said, 'Will you not assist me?' 'I will,' Ranald replied, 'though no other man in the Highlands should draw his sword.' After that, most of the MacDonalds agreed to join; but Charles's troubles were not yet over, for the chief of the strong Cameron clan, Donald Cameron of Lochiel, also advised him to return to France. Charles refused to follow this advice:

' "In a few days," said he, "with the few friends that I have, I will erect the royal standard, and proclaim to the people of Britain that Charles Stuart is come over to claim the crown of his ancestors, to win it, or to perish in the attempt: Lochiel, who, my father has often told me, was our firmest friend, may stay at home and learn from the newspapers the fate of his prince." '

' "No," said Lochiel, "I'll share the fate of my prince; and so shall every man over whom nature or fortune hath given me any power." '

Cameron of Lochiel

Now that some support was assured, arrangements were made for the standard to be raised at Glenfinnan on 19 August, the various leaders went off to raise their men, and the ship that had brought the adventurers from France left the coast. In the meantime, the first fighting had taken place. News of the landing had reached the government and two companies of the Royal Scots were sent to the support of the garrison at Fort William, but they still had eight miles to go when some Highlanders appeared on the other side of a bridge which they had to cross. The officer in command did not know that he was faced by only about a dozen men and ordered a retreat; but, as they marched back, they were attacked by more and more Highlanders and were finally forced to surrender.

Prince Charles moved to Glenfinnan and awaited the arrival of Cameron of Lochiel before raising the standard.

The monument of Glenfinnan which marks Prince Charles' landing place

Here is how one of the Prince's followers described what happened:

'The Camerons advanced in two lines (each of them three men deep). Between the lines were the soldiers taken on the 16th, marching as prisoners without their arms. Charles, elated with the sight of such a clan (for the Camersons are said to have been 700 or 800 men that day) proceeded immediately to erect the standard.

The Marquis of Tullibardine unfurled the standard; and, supported by a man on each side, held the staff till the *manifest* and *commission of regency* were read.'

Two days later the Prince heard that a reward of £30,000 had been offered for his capture and promptly offered a reward of £30 for the capture of George II! This was later changed to £30,000 also; and the little army set off for the Lowlands. In the next section we will follow them on their journey.

From Glenfinnan to Edinburgh
In the middle of the eighteenth century news travelled slowly, but the government got to know of Prince Charlie's landing before the end of July, and on 8 August General Sir John Cope, the Commander-in-Chief in Scotland, gave orders for stores and men to be got together ready for an advance into the Highlands. He was hopeful that he would be able to scatter the rebel army before it reached the Lowlands. On the same day as the standard was raised at Glenfinnan he left Edinburgh for Stirling, and from there he set off for the north with about 1,400 infantry and some artillery. It was thought that cavalry would not be much use in mountainous country, so they were left behind to guard Edinburgh and the crossing places over the River Forth near Stirling. The government troops headed for Fort Augustus, but Cope was warned that the Jacobites would attack him at Corryarrick Pass if he tried

to cross it, and, sure enough, Charles's men took up their position on the top of the Pass the next day. (You can follow these movements on the map on the endpapers.) What would you have done in Sir John Cope's place—tried to attack up the Pass, or gone back to Stirling? Actually, he didn't do either of these things. He turned to his right and marched first to Inverness and then to Aberdeen, where he got ships to carry his army back to Dunbar, in the hope that he would arrive near Edinburgh before the Prince. You can probably see why this was not a good plan—it left the road to the Lowlands open to the Jacobite army, which now moved quickly southwards towards the capital without fear of attack.

The first large town to fall into the Prince's hands was Perth, where he was joined by more supporters and by one person in particular who was to play a very important part in the rebellion—Lord George Murray. He was a younger brother of 'Duke James' and 'Duke William' and had fought in the risings of 1715 and 1719; but, having received a royal pardon, he settled down on an estate in Perthshire and decided only at the last moment to join the Prince. Though Charles made him Lieutenant-General of the army along with the Duke of Perth he never trusted him completely because he had accepted a pardon from George I, and this often caused a great deal of trouble. Here is how another Jacobite officer described Lord George:

'He was tall and *robust* and brave in the highest degree; and always the first to rush sword in hand into the midst of the enemy. He used to say, when we advanced to the charge, "I do not ask you, my lads, to go before, but merely to follow me". . . . He slept little, was continually occupied with all manner of details, and was altogether most indefatigable, combining and directing alone all our operations: in a word, he was the only person capable of conducting our army. . . . However, he was not without

41

his defects: proud, haughty, blunt, and *imperious*, he wished
to have the exclusive ordering of everything; and, feeling
his superiority, he would listen to no advice.'

From this description we can guess that the Prince and Lord
George would not get on very well, especially when things
were going badly for the Jacobite army.

Leaving Perth, Charles and his men crossed the Forth at
the Fords of Frew and reached the outskirts of Edinburgh on
16 September. The cavalry which was supposed to guard the
crossing-places had retreated to Coltbridge, just outside

Edinburgh, but, when the Highlanders appeared they fled, after firing a few shots. They continued their retreat beyond the city, and in the darkness one of them was unfortunate enough to stumble into a shallow coalpit. The clatter which he and his horse made convinced the others that the Highland army was right behind them, and caused an even greater panic than before! The name given to this skirmish was 'The Canter of Coltbridge'.

The Prince's approach caused great excitement in Edinburgh. Two-thirds of the men, we are told, were for the government, and two-thirds of the ladies were for the Prince! A body of volunteers was formed to defend the city, and one of them wrote later, 'In one house on the south side of the street there was a row of windows, full of ladies, who appeared to enjoy our march to danger with much levity and mirth!' Though Edinburgh did have walls on three sides the Town Council knew that the city could not be defended and they sent a deputation to the Jacobite army; but, while it was away, news came that Cope's transports had appeared off Dunbar! In the hope that he might get to Edinburgh in time to save them the Council sent another letter to the Prince, asking a little more time to discuss what was to be done; but the messengers that carried back Charles's refusal were closely followed by Cameron of Lochiel and his men, and, when the Netherbow gate was opened for the messengers' coach, the Highlanders rushed in 'with a hideous yell' and the capital was taken. The rest of the army followed soon after, and Charles took up his residence in the Palace of Holyroodhouse. On his way there he went through the King's Park, which was full of people who had come to see him pass, and one of those who were there that day has left us this description:

'He was in the prime of youth, tall and handsome, of a fair complexion . . . he wore the Highland dress, that is, a tartan short coat without the plaid, a blue bonnet on his head, and on his breast the star of the order of St Andrew.'

Later the same day the Prince got the *Heralds* and *Pursuivants* to proclaim his father James VIII of Scotland, as had been done at Perth and Dundee, and the same writer says:

'The populace huzzaed; and a number of ladies in the windows strained their voices with acclamation, and their arms with waving white handkerchiefs in honour of the day. These demonstrations of joy were chiefly confined to one sex; few gentlemen were to be seen on the streets, or in the windows; and many shewed their dislike by a stubborn silence.'

On 20 September the Prince and his men left Edinburgh again, this time marching eastwards to meet General Cope's army which was advancing from Dunbar.

The Battle of Prestonpans

As the armies advanced towards one another, the two leaders must have thought a lot about the coming battle, for they knew that a great deal depended on it. If Prince Charlie lost, it would be the end of his attempt to put his father on the throne of Britain; if he won, it would give him control of the whole of Scotland, as there were no other troops in the country to oppose him. The royalist and the Jacobite forces finally came in sight of each other near the town of Mussel-burgh, and, if you look at the map on page 45 you will see what happened when they did so.

As soon as Sir John Cope heard that the Highland army was near, he took up a very good position with the sea behind him and the right wing of his army protected by the ten-foot high walls which surrounded the grounds of Preston House. There was a deep ditch and a wide stretch of marshy ground in front of his men too, so that although Lord George Murray led the Jacobite forces to the top of a hill near Tranent, where they could look down on their enemies, you can see that it would

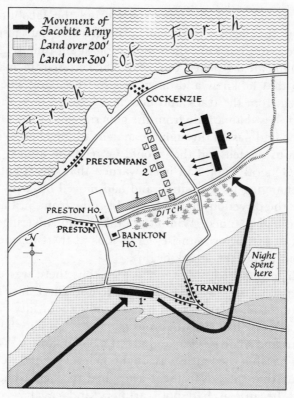

Plan of the battle of Prestonpans

have been very dangerous for them to attack the government troops as long as they stayed in that position. Lord George's *aide-de-camp*, the *Chevalier* Johnstone, tells us that they spent the afternoon scouting around Cope's position, and the more they looked at it the more worried they got, as they could not see any way of attacking it without heavy losses.

At last Lord George decided that the best way was to lead the Highlanders down on to the level ground between the marsh and the sea, and then, of course, Sir John would have to turn his men to face them, and so give up his strong position.

45

Darkness fell soon after they started and the Jacobite army slept in the fields, from which the harvest had just been gathered, until 4 a.m., then moved on again quietly, guided by a man called Robert Anderson. They crossed the marsh by a path that he knew and dawn was just breaking when they emerged from the track and marched forward onto the hard ground, less than a mile from the government army. Once all the men had passed through the marsh, all they had to do was to turn to the left and they would be ready to attack. Meanwhile General Cope had been warned that the Highlanders were changing their position and had moved his army round to face the direction that they would come from, just as Lord George had planned. While the ranks stand shivering in the chill mist just before sunrise, let us look at the two sides for a moment before the attack begins.

Both armies had about 2,500 men, but there was quite a difference in the way they were made up. The Prince's army was almost all infantry and he had only about fifty cavalry, whereas Cope had six squadrons of cavalry (about 560 men), six guns and some *mortars*, and about 2,000 infantry. When we remember that the battle was fought on level ground we would imagine that the government army had the better chance of success because it had both artillery and cavalry—do you know why? Unluckily for General Cope, however, his cavalry were the same that had already run away from the Highlanders at Coltbridge and Leith; and he had only a few gunners for his artillery, who fled as soon as the battle started. To make matters worse, his infantry were badly trained and had no experience of the Highland method of fighting, so you see that Prince Charlie really had the advantage in the coming battle. Here is how a royalist supporter described what happened:

'The ground between the two armies was an extensive corn field, plain and level, without a bush or tree, and the ground was covered with a thick stubble, which rustled under the feet of the Highlanders as they ran on, speaking and muttering in a manner that expressed their fierceness and rage. When they set out the mist was very thick; but before they got halfway, the sun rose, dispelled the mist, and showed the armies to each other. As the left wing of the rebel army had moved before the right, the Camerons came up directly opposite the cannon. The people employed to work the cannon fled instantly. Colonel Whiteford fired five of the six *field pieces* with his own hand. . . . The line seemed to shake, but the men kept going on at a

The battle of Prestonpans

great pace. The *dragoons* received some fire and immediately wheeled about, rode over the artillery guard, and fled. . . . When the dragoons on the right of the King's army gave way, the Highlanders advanced against the foot, firing as they went on. The soldiers, terrified to see the cannon taken and the dragoons put to flight, gave their fire, it is said, without orders. . . . The Highlanders threw down their musquets, drew their swords, and ran on; the line of foot broke. . . . In a very few minutes after the first cannon was fired, the whole army, both horse and foot, were put to flight; none of the soldiers attempted to load

47

their pieces again, and not one bayonet was stained with blood.'

As you can see from this description, the battle was won by the speed and ferocity of the Highlanders' attack and was lost because Cope's infantry were badly trained and because his cavalry and artillery were useless. His army lost about 300 men killed and about 1,500 taken prisoner, and the Prince's army had about twenty-five or thirty killed and about seventy wounded. After the battle the Highland officers did all they could to see that Cope's wounded as well as their own were properly cared for—a great contrast to what happened later

A cartoon of Sir John Cope's arrival at Berwick

after the battle of Culloden.

Prestonpans was an important victory for the Prince, for, as we have seen, there was no other government army in Scotland, so that he was now in control of the whole country, except for Edinburgh, Stirling and Dumbarton castles and the forts in the Highlands. Also, some of those who had not joined him at first, such as Lord Lovat, the chief of the Frasers, were now ready to do so. Unfortunately, its most important effect was to give the Prince the mistaken idea that his Highland troops were practically unbeatable; and we shall see that this was going to be one cause of his final defeat.

4   The Invasion of England

'Immediately after the defeat of Cope, six thousand Dutch troops arrived in England, and three battalions of guards, with seven regiments of infantry, were recalled from Flanders for the defence of the kingdom. They forthwith began their march to the North, under the command of General Wade, who received orders to assemble an army. The Duke of Cumberland arrived from the Netherlands, and was followed by another detachment of dragoons and infantry. The *train bands* of London were reviewed by his Majesty: the county regiments were completed: the volunteers in different parts of the kingdom employed themselves industriously in the exercise of arms; and the whole English nation seemed to rise up as one man against this formidable invader.'

The paragraph which you have just read comes from a history which was written by the novelist Tobias Smollett. (Do you know any of the books that he wrote? And do you remember why troops had to be brought back from Europe?) This paragraph shows us how alarmed the government and many of the people of Britain must have been at the news of Sir John Cope's defeat, and what quick action was taken to crush the rebellion.

Meanwhile the Prince had returned to Edinburgh, where he stayed from 22 September to 31 October. This enabled more supporters to join him, such as the Earl of Kilmarnock and his son; Lord Balmerino; MacPherson of Cluny; the Chief of MacKinnon, and about 2,500 men of different clans. The Marquis d'Aiguilles, the French ambassador, also arrived; and, about this time, four French ships bringing guns and stores. The army was thus increased in size, but you can probably think of at least two reasons why such a long stay in

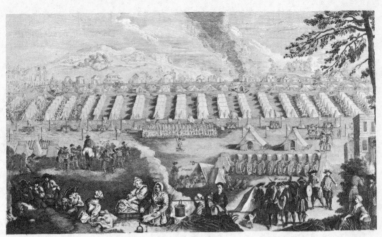
An imaginary picture of the Jacobite camp at Edinburgh

Edinburgh was unwise. From the two quotations which are printed below, you can see what the Prince did during his stay in the capital, and you can see also that things were not going as smoothly as they might have been.

'The Prince lived in Edinburgh with Great Splendour and Magnificence, had Every morning a numerous Court of his Officers. After he had held a Councill, he dinn'd with his principall officers in publick, where their was always a Crowd of all sorts of people to See him dine. After dinner he rode out Attended by his life guards and review'd his Army, where their was always a great number of Spectators in Coaches and on horseback. After the review, he Came to the Abey, where he received the ladies of fashion that came to his drawing-room. Then he Sup'd in publick, and Generaly their was musick at Supper, and a Ball afterwards.'

'The Prince in this Councill used Always first to declare what he was for, and then he Ask'd Every bodys opinion in their turn. Their was one third of the Councill . . . always

Confirmed whatever the Prince Said. The other two thirds, who thought that Kings and Princes . . . were not altogether infallible and that this Prince was no more so than others, beg'd leave to differ from him, when they Could give Sufficient reasons for their difference of opinion. . . . The Prince Could not bear to hear any body differ . . . from him, and took a dislike to Every body that did.'

At last it was decided that an advance into England must be made in order to give the southern Jacobites a chance to come to the Prince's support, so the army packed up and left Edinburgh on 1 November. Charles wanted to march straight to Newcastle to attack General Wade, who, you remember, had been ordered to collect an army there. But the chiefs persuaded him that it would be better if they advanced down the west coast so that the Jacobites of northern England could join them, and then Wade would be more easily defeated. In the end, as you can see from the map on the endpaper, one part of the army set off by Kelso and Jedburgh in order to make General Wade think that they were going to attack Newcastle and so prevent him from moving his men; while the other part marched straight to Carlisle. The first group turned to the west before they reached the border, and the two parts joined forces again just north of Carlisle.

It did not look as though it would be easy to capture the town, for it was defended by a castle and encircled by walls; and, since everyone expected that General Wade would march to its assistance at once, the Jacobite army was marched to Brampton to be ready for him when he came. As you can imagine, the people of Carlisle were alarmed at the appearance of the Highland army. The mayor was more alarmed than anyone, for he had just received three very unwelcome letters! Two of them were from the Jacobites, one demanding billets for 13,000 men and the other warning him what would happen if the gates of the town were not opened to their army, while the third was from General Wade, saying that he was sure that the Highlanders would not attack the town, but wishing the garrison 'all imaginable success'! As soon as the Prince realised that there was no danger from Wade, half the army was sent back to Carlisle, and the siege was started on the evening of 13 November. Here is an account of what happened, written by one of the besiegers:

'The trenches were opened before Carlisle on Wednesday [and] on Friday morning the batteries were erected. . . . All that time the cannon and small arms from both city and castle *played* most furiously; but with no loss to the besiegers other than of a French gunner and a private man killed. The Duke of Perth and the Marquis of Tullibardine wrought at the trenches in their shirts, though the weather was so excessively cold, that none of the army but the Highlanders could easily endure it. On Friday, when the cannon began to play, and the scaling-ladders were brought forward, a white flag was hung out, and the city offered to surrender. The Prince answered that the city had no terms to expect unless the castle surrendered at the same time. When this answer was reported, Colonel Durand [the commander] consented to surrender the castle also.'

When Wade heard that the siege had really started, he set out from Newcastle, but his men were delayed by deep snow; and he turned back when he heard that the town had been captured. If Charles had known how miserable Wade's men were after spending all night in the snow on the open moor with hardly any provisions, they might have marched to Newcastle themselves and won another easy victory, for many of Wade's regular soldiers were terrified at the idea of meeting the Highlanders, and the Dutch and German troops who were also in his army did not much care which king ruled Britain.

Instead of doing this, the Highland army marched south again. As we know, one of the reasons for crossing the border was to give the English Jacobites a chance to join the Prince, and, though only two gentlemen had done so in Northumberland, Charles was certain that more would appear as they advanced. In thinking this he was quite wrong, for, though the people seemed friendly enough, and greeted him 'with the loudest acclamations of joy', as they did at Preston, very few were prepared to leave their jobs and their homes to join the army. One of the Jacobite officers wrote:

'The road betwixt Preston and Wigan was crouded with people standing at their doors to see the army go by, and they generaly profes'd to wish the Princes army Success, but if arms was offer'd to them and they were desir'd to Go along with the army thay all declined, and Said they did not Understand fighting.'

The Prince seemed to think that everything was going well, but his chief officers realised that matters were now getting serious. They had been joined by no more than 200 men, mostly from Manchester, and the French had not landed to help them, as they had hoped. Worse still, General Wade's

St. Anne's Square, Manchester. (The Highland army camped here on their way south.)

army was behind them, another one under the King's son, the Duke of Cumberland was in front, and a third was being formed to defend London. (This force was being collected on Finchley Common, but if you look at the picture on page 55 you will probably think that the Guards were not in a very great hurry to get there! Ask your art teacher to show you some other pictures done by this artist.) Most of the Jacobite leaders felt that the sensible thing to do was to return to Scotland, where they might raise more men; but at last it was decided to go on to Derby, so that no one could say that they had not gone far enough to encourage the English to join them or the French to send an expedition. Lord George Murray tricked the Duke of Cumberland into thinking that the army intended to march into Wales, and when the government troops moved in that direction, the Highlanders had a clear road to Derby. London now lay right ahead, only four days' march away!

Horace Walpole, writing to a friend, exclaimed what he thought had happened.

'The Duke, from some strange want of *intelligence, lay* last week for four-and-twenty hours under arms at Stone, in Staffordshire, expecting the rebels every moment, while they were marching in all haste to Derby. The news of this threw the town [London] into great consternation.'

Jacobite proclamations appeared on the walls of the capital. It is said that this was done by a man who went round the streets carrying a large bundle; inside the bundle was a small boy, who, every now and then, would pop out, paste up a proclamation, and slip back into the bundle before he was spotted. People began to try to withdraw their money from the banks, and to prevent too much from being withdrawn (which would have caused trouble for the government) the banks paid them in sixpences, which, of course, took so long to count that not much could be paid out! Some writers even say that the sixpences were heated red-hot to make them hard to pick up.

Naturally, none of the Jacobite army at Derby knew about this, and all but Charles himself were alarmed at the position they were in. It is true that they could easily have reached London before the armies of Wade and Cumberland; it is possible that they would have defeated the force that was guarding the capital; but after that, what then? The Prince's only chance of success would have been if the people of London had taken his side and overthrown King George. If they had not done so, then he could not have held the capital with his small army, or defeated the two approaching armies, both of which were nearly twice as big as his. Charles, of course, was sure that the people would take his side, though, as we know, very few had done so up to that time. Horace Walpole continued his letter:

Hogarth's famous picture of the March of the Guards to Finchley.

'Here in London, the aversion to them is amazing: on some thoughts of the King's going to an encampment at Finchley, the weavers not only offered him a thousand men, but the whole body of the Law formed themselves into a little army, under the command of Lord Chief-Justice Willes, and were to have done duty at St. James's, to guard the royal family in the King's absence.'

Swarkstone Bridge, Derby. (This is thought to be the most southerly point reached by the Jacobite army.)

But Prince Charlie did not know this either, and he was very surprised when Lord George met him the morning after they had arrived in Derby, and told him that his officers thought that a retreat must be started at once.

You can imagine how angry Charles must have felt. At the Council of War which was held, Lord Elcho tells us that:

'The Prince heard all arguments with the greatest impatience, fell into a passion and gave most of the Gentlemen that had Spoke very Abusive Language, and said that

56

they had a mind to betray him. . . . He Continued all that day positive he would march to London [but] at Night the Prince Sent for them and told them he consented to go to Scotland. And at the same time he told them that for the future he would have no more Councills, for he would neither ask nor take their Advice, and he was as good as his word.'

So on 6 December—'Black Friday' as it was called—the retreat began. The Prince was sullen and spoke to hardly anyone but his Irish officers; though he had always been one of the first to be up and on the move when they were coming south, now he stayed in his lodgings until about 9 a.m. every day, and then came out and rode off to join the leading troops. This was very hard on Lord George who had offered to command the rearguard all the way back to the Border, for of course he had to wait for the Prince, and his men could not move as fast on foot as Charles could on horseback. He did not seem to realise that there was great danger that General Wade would cross over and block their return to Scotland, and they would then be caught between his army and that of the Duke of Cumberland. The people who, a few days before, had *illuminated* their windows and cheered their advance now became hostile, and stragglers from the army were sure to be ill-treated or even killed. The Duke of Cumberland wrote to the Duke of Newcastle: 'As they have so many of our prisoners in their hands I did not care to put them [the Jacobite prisoners] to death, but I have encouraged the country people to do it.'

They reached Manchester on 9 December and Wigan on the 10th, by which time Wade had got only as far as Wakefield, so they were safe from that danger at least; but the Duke of Cumberland was still pursuing with all his cavalry and 1,000 infantry, some of them on horseback too. Preston was reached on the 11th, Lancaster on the 13th and Kendal on the 15th, a day's rest being given the men at each of these

c

places, but now they were faced with the crossing of Shap Fell. Of course, this was easy for the Highlanders, but the army had to get its baggage over too, and the country people had been digging holes in the roads and blocking them with boulders to delay their retreat. At Kendal Lord George asked O'Sullivan, the Quartermaster, to have the baggage put into light carts instead of the heavy waggons they had been using, but O'Sullivan either forgot or did not bother to do so. As a result, after they had gone only about three miles, one of the waggons stuck on a steep hill, and everyone had to push to help the horses. This happened several times, and, as it was a day of pouring rain, they must all have been very tired and thoroughly miserable by nightfall. The next day they got as many light carts as they could and transferred their baggage into them, but the rivers were so swollen with the rain that they were almost impossible to cross even with the light carts. At one very steep hill the horses could not pull those that were loaded with cannon balls, so Lord George gave his men six-pence each to carry one with them to the top of Shap, which they did, tied up in a corner of their plaids. When they got there, they found that the main part of the army had eaten nearly all the food, so they toasted slices of cheese on the points of their *claymores* and ate them between pieces of bread.

Lord George's troubles were far from over even then, for he found that he was now expected to take over the care of the artillery as well as the baggage. To make matters worse, the various delays had allowed the Duke of Cumberland to catch up with them, and scouting parties of dragoons were watching them all the time. The baggage was sent on to Penrith, but Lord George remained at Clifton, for he was sure that they would soon be attacked. A message was sent to the Prince asking for 1,000 men to come to the help of the rearguard. The men were not sent, but soon a large body of enemy cavalry appeared and drew up on the open moor in two lines, and, about sunset, Cumberland sent in three detachments to attack the enclosures where Lord George had placed his men. The cavalry dismounted and advanced, but by now it was almost dark, and each side fired at the other's musket flashes. At last, led by Lord George and their chief, both shouting 'Claymore' at the tops of their voices, the Macphersons charged the dragoons and drove them off after a sharp fight in which about a dozen were killed on each side. The rearguard then withdrew to Penrith, and this little action at Clifton, (the last to be fought on English soil), put an end to the pursuit for the time being and allowed the army to reach Carlisle in safety.

As you can see, the Prince had done very little to help his general during the retreat—in fact, you could make quite a list of the ways in which he had made things more difficult for him. Now, when they reached Carlisle, he ordered that 400 men should be left behind as a garrison so that he could say

The Duke of Cumberland accepting the surrender of Carlisle

that he held at least one English town, even though nearly everyone advised him not to do so, as they could not possibly hold out against Cumberland. Sure enough, the Duke brought up heavy cannons, and after about two days the

The execution of two prisoners after the capture of Carlisle

garrison was forced to surrender. Later, the officers were hanged and the men were sentenced to seven years in the *Plantations*.

The army stayed for only one day at Carlisle and on 20 December they crossed the Esk safely. Lord George described the scene like this:

'We were a hundred men abreast, and it was a very fine show; the water was big, and took most of the men breast-high. When I was near cross the river, I believe there were two thousand men in the water at once; there was nothing seen but their heads and shoulders; but there was no danger, for we had caused try the water, and the ford was good, and Highlanders will pass a water where horses will not. . . . The pipers began to play so soon as we passed, and the men all danced reels, which in a moment dried them.'

He had every reason to be pleased with their return, for it was mainly due to him that it had been done safely. He had out-marched and out-manoeuvred the commanders of two armies, both much larger than the Jacobite one, and even his enemies admired what he had accomplished. 'I don't know who has the command of these people's affairs', wrote Lord Cobham, 'but this I can assert, that they have not committed one mistake since they came into the kingdom.'

In the march from Carlisle to Derby and back again, a distance of 240 miles, the Prince had lost only about forty men, including those killed or captured at Clifton, which was fewer than General Wade had lost in his march from Newcastle to Hexham. Who knows what he might have done with a larger army that had proper cavalry and artillery!

5 The Retreat

Christmas Day 1745 cannot have been a very happy day for
the citizens of Glasgow, for, on that day, the vanguard of the
Highland army came marching in from the south. They had
left Carlisle on 20 December, and now the people were
wondering just what they might expect from these ranks of

One of the main streets in Glasgow in the eighteenth century

wild-looking men.

They had some cause for alarm. Glasgow had never been
friendly to the Stuarts, for the people were afraid that a Stuart
king would want to break the Treaty of Union with England
which was helping to make the town prosperous. They had
even raised ten companies of men to fight the Earl of Mar in

62

1715; and then, in September 1745, the Prince had demanded a loan of £15,000, which, after a good deal of trouble, they had managed to reduce to £5,000 in money and £500 in goods. Now they had no idea what new demands the Jacobites might make. As it happened, they did not have to wait long to find out; but, in the meantime, the Prince arrived on the 26th at the head of the clans, and the men were billeted in the public and private houses of the city. They must have been quiet and peaceable, just as they had been on their march through England, for there are no stories of looting or ill-usage of the citizens: but two days later the magistrates and chief inhabitants were told by the Quartermaster of the Highland army that the city must supply them with 6,000 cloth coats, 12,000 linen shirts, 6,000 pairs of shoes, 6,000 bonnets and 6,000 pairs of tartan hose. When the magistrates protested, they were told that they were rebels, and, if they did not produce the goods, the Prince would make them 'an example of his just severity, that would strike terror in other places'. It is said that it was the 'gentle Lochiel', chief of the Camerons, who persuaded Charles not to *sack* the city; and, in gratitude, the citizens decided that, ever afterwards, the bells should be rung whenever Lochiel visited Glasgow. We have no written record of this decision anywhere, but the custom is still carried out to the present day. After this, it is not surprising to find Provost Andrew Cochrane writing that the Prince:

'appeared four times publickly on our streets, without acclamation or one huzza; no ringing of bells, or smallest respect or acknowledgement paid him by the meanest inhabitant. Our very ladys had not the curiosity to go near him, and declined going to a ball held by his chiefs.'

The Prince stayed at Shawfield House, near the West *Port*, and there he met the youngest daughter of John Walkinshaw of Barrowfield. This was an odd coincidence, because John Walkinshaw had had a share in the rescue of Charles's mother, the Princess Clementina, that you read about at the beginning of this book. As a reward, when Mr and Mrs Walkinshaw's daughter was born in Rome, the Princess gave the baby her own name and became her godmother. Later, Clementina Walkinshaw was to join the Prince in Europe, and may even have been married to him.

Miss Clementina Walkinshaw

Dugald Graham, the Glasgow pedlar and bellman, has left us this rhyming picture of the Highland army:

The shot was rusted in the gun,
    Their swords from scabbards would not *twin*;
Their count'nance fierce as a wild bear,
    Out o'er their eyes hang down their hair . . .
Their beards were turned black and brown,

The like was ne'er seen in that town,
  Some of them did barefoot run
   Minded no mire nor stoney groun';
  But when shaven, drest and clothed again,
   They turned to be like other men.

The army left Glasgow on 3 January 1746, and the citizens must have been glad to see them go, even though they took two merchants with them as securities that they would get some of the clothing that could not be supplied in time. Provost Cochrane and his brother-in-law, Bailie George Murdoch, spent six months in London (which cost them the sum of £472 11s 8½d in expenses), trying to get the government to pay Glasgow £10,000 compensation for her losses. They were successful at last, and the citizens were so pleased with their provost that they agreed that Cotton Street should be re-named Cochrane Street in his honour.

The Battle of Falkirk

Can you think of one or two reasons why the Prince went to Glasgow instead of to Edinburgh after his return from England, especially when he knew that the Glasgow people did not like the Stuart family? One of your answers might be that, while the Highland army was in England, Edinburgh had been recaptured by government troops, and by 10 January 1746, there were twelve battalions there, commanded by Lieutenant-General Hawley. The General was not a very nice person, and, because he treated his soldiers so severely, they nicknamed him 'Lord Chief Justice'. Do you know why?

While the government troops were gathering at Edinburgh, reinforcements for the Jacobite army were being collected at Perth. There were Frasers and Mackintoshes, Farquharsons and Mackenzies, MacDonalds, Camerons and MacGregors; and Lord John Drummond, who commanded a French regiment called the Royal Scots, had landed with about 800 men

Lord John Drummond

in November. There were now about 3,000–4,000 men waiting to join the Prince, and, when the two groups met at Stirling, Charles commanded an army of about 8,000 men. Lord John had also brought some artillery with him, which was lucky, because the Highland army had left all but three of their guns at Carlisle, and, of course, they needed big guns to besiege Stirling Castle.

This task was given to Colonel Grant, who was in charge of the artillery, but, as you can guess from the picture on page 67, it was very difficult to find a place to put the guns so that their fire would reach the top of the rock. Colonel Grant did find one, but the townspeople all complained that their houses

Stirling Castle

would be knocked down when the firing began, so the Prince asked another officer to find a different place. This person was M. Mirabel de Gordon, and you can see from his name that he was part French and part Scots. Unluckily, he did not know much about gunnery, and 'Mr Admirable' (as the Highlanders called him) chose a very unsuitable position indeed. The siege went on until after the battle of Falkirk, but, as it is easy to guess what happened, we may as well read the Chevalier Johnstone's description of it now:

'M. Mirabelle, with a childish impatience immediately began a very brisk fire, but it was of short duration and produced very little effect on the batteries of the Castle, which being more elevated than ours, the enemy could see even the buckles of the shoes of our artillerymen. As their fire commanded ours, our guns were immediately *dismounted*, and in less than half an hour we were obliged to abandon our battery altogether.'

On 13 January the first part of General Hawley's army set off towards Stirling, and was soon followed by the remainder. Only part of the Highland army was besieging Stirling Castle and Lord George Murray was at Falkirk with five of the clan regiments, so he advanced at once to Linlithgow to meet the government troops, hoping for a chance to attack them. When he saw that this was impossible he rejoined the Prince at Bannockburn, and General Hawley then occupied Falkirk. Of course, the Jacobites expected to be attacked at once, but, when no attack came for two days, Lord George suggested that they should do the attacking themselves. As a first step, it was decided to take the army on to a high piece of moorland about a mile from Hawley's camp. To distract attention from this move, Lord John Drummond, leading part of his own regiment and other troops, began marching along the main road from Bannockburn to Falkirk. The main part of the army then headed for the high ground by a roundabout route.

General Hawley, who was staying some distance away, had visited the camp that morning, but he never dreamed that the Highlanders would dare to attack him, so, when news was brought of the Jacobite advance, he did not bother to return, but just sent an order that the men were to put on their equipment. A little later, however, a message reached the General that the enemy were heading for the high ground above his army, and he galloped back to the camp without even waiting to put on his hat.

When he saw what was happening, he at once ordered his cavalry to advance up the slope, followed by the infantry and artillery; and the leading regiments of the two armies reached the high ground about the same time. The MacDonalds were on the right of the Jacobite army and so arrived on the hill first, so they advanced very slowly in order to let the other regiments get into line with them. On the other side, Hawley's infantry, breathless from climbing the hill, formed up on the right of the cavalry. The artillery of both armies did not advance quickly enough, and so did not get into the battle at all.

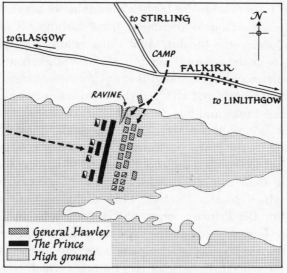

Plan of the battle of Falkirk

Now, if you look at the map on this page you will see what the battlefield looked like. The right wing of the Prince's army was protected by a marsh and its left by a ravine, but the Stewarts and Camerons on the left were *outflanked* by the royal infantry on the other side of the ravine, which was going to have an important effect on the battle. It was a dull and stormy day, and, when the armies were forming up, a high wind began to drive rain into the faces of the royal troops, soaking the cartridges of their muskets, so that many missed fire when the attack began.

Even before all his men were in line, General Hawley ordered his cavalry to advance, for he was sure that the Highlanders would not stand a charge; but Lord George, who commanded the right wing, waited till the cavalry were only ten yards away and then ordered his men to fire. About eighty of the horsemen were killed at once, and most of the rest turned and fled, while those who did stay to fight were soon driven off.

Though Lord George did his best, he could not prevent two of the three MacDonald regiments from dashing off after the cavalry, and so the Jacobite right wing became scattered. The regiments in the centre, having fired their muskets at the flying cavalry, could not reload them in the heavy rain, so they drew their swords and charged the royal infantry on the left, which also broke and fled. The only part of the royal army to put up a good resistance were the troops on the right, who were protected by the ravine in front of them. They now marched up the hill to their left and fired at the Highlanders who were pursuing their comrades, helped by one of the cavalry regiments which had re-formed. This might have been quite serious for the Prince's army, but reserves were brought up from the Jacobite second line, and the royal troops retreated.

This battle was not as complete a victory as the Jacobites would have liked, because of two mistakes which were made before the fighting began. As we have seen, Hawley's men were allowed to outflank the Highlanders on the right, and so they were able to attack the advancing Highlanders from the side. The second mistake was that the Prince did not appoint any special officers to command the different parts of the army before the battle began, though Lord George had asked him twice to do so. As a result, there was no commanding officer on the left who could have seen what was happening in time. Even Lord George himself had only been told to lead the front line troops, which meant that he commanded the right wing. As he himself said, if officers had been properly appointed, the fighting would not have lasted ten minutes.

In spite of these mistakes, it was a Jacobite victory. They lost about fifty killed and about seventy wounded, while Hawley's army had perhaps 300 killed and 500 taken prisoner. It is said that the General was so angry that he broke his sword against the market cross in Falkirk. His army had to suffer a good deal of jeering from the Jacobite supporters when they returned to Edinburgh; and, though the General was not blamed for his defeat, his place was taken by the Duke of Cumberland, who arrived in Edinburgh on 30 January.

The Duke of Cumberland

The Highlands again

What would you have done in Prince Charlie's place the morning after Falkirk? Some of his officers thought that, since General Hawley was defeated and their army had got many more recruits, it would be a good idea to march to London again; others said that Hawley should be pursued; and a third lot thought that the siege of Stirling Castle should be continued. The correct decision would have been to pursue Hawley (can you see why?). Unluckily it was decided to carry on the siege of the Castle. Even if they could have captured it, the Castle would have been of no use to them, but, as we have seen on page 167, the attempt of 'Mr Admirable' ended in failure, and Lord George Murray and the clan chiefs decided that a retreat should be made to the Highlands.

The trouble was that, with the siege of the Castle going on, the clansmen had little to do, and some of them, it was

An earlier picture of Stirling Castle

thought, had taken the chance of slipping off home. Cumberland had also received reinforcements, and it was felt that they had little chance of defeating him; while, if they went to the Highlands, they could get more recruits and could spend the time capturing the government forts.

Prince Charlie was against the retreat, of course. He said that it would end any hope of getting French help and that the enemy would be cheered up by the sight of the Highlanders returning to the mountains—worse still, they would need to leave their heavy cannon behind. For once, he was probably right, but he could not persuade the chiefs to change their minds, and the retreat began on 1 February 1746.

The Duke of Cumberland had already advanced to Linlithgow, so Lord George withdrew to Bannockburn, where the Prince had gone after the battle of Falkirk. It was decided that the army should all collect at 9 a.m. at St Ninian's, outside Stirling, and start their march northwards, with Lord George in command of the rearguard as usual; but for some reason the army set off by itself at dawn, in great confusion, leaving carts and cannon behind as they went. As Lord George made his way to the meeting-place he was alarmed by a terrific explosion, which was the accidental blowing up of the gunpowder which had been stored in St Ninian's church; and, when he got to the appointed place, of course there was no one there. You can guess that he was in a very bad mood when he finally crossed the Forth and headed for the north, and when a council of war was held at Crieff there was a great deal of argument and unpleasantness. Finally, it was decided that he should lead one part of the army northwards by the coast road, and that the Prince should lead the other part through the Highlands. (You can follow this on the map on the endpaper.)

The two parts finally reached Inverness on 21 February.

Fort George and Inverness in 1744

73

Fort George and Fort Augustus were both captured soon afterwards, and, though 'Mr Admirable' failed to take Fort William, a raid on the government posts in Atholl led by Lord George ended with thirty of them being captured. Things seemed to be looking up for the little Jacobite army, but the government troops under the Duke of Cumberland had reached Aberdeen on 25 February, and they had advanced to Nairn by 14 April. The end of the adventure was in sight.

6 The End of the Adventure

The Night March

Now that the two armies were so close to each other, it became more and more obvious to everyone except Charles that things were not going well. Just when they needed money most, the Jacobites' finances ran out, and the men were without pay. Even worse than this, supplies of food and clothing were also very short, as the Prince's Secretary, who had looked after these things, had become ill and had been replaced by another man who was not nearly so efficient. As we have seen, the Jacobite leaders had never agreed very well, and now these disagreements became even more serious. Lastly, Lord George Murray had chosen a very strong position for the army to occupy when the government forces arrived, but this was changed by O'Sullivan, who decided on a piece of open moorland near Culloden House, which gave all the advantages to Cumberland's men.

Perhaps it was because he disliked the chosen battlefield so much that Lord George agreed to the Prince's plan to attack Cumberland's camp at Nairn on the night of the 15th April. This was really a very difficult thing to do, for Nairn is about eight miles from Culloden, and not only had the whole Jacobite army to get there unseen and unheard, but part of it had to get round to the east side of the town and attack the rear of Cumberland's camp while the other part attacked the front. All this had to be done between about 7 p.m. and 2 a.m. This may seem to be plenty of time for an eight-mile march, but we must remember that a large body of men can move only very slowly at night, and that it would take a long time to get the two parts of the army into position for the attack.

The whole attempt was almost called off before it started, when it was found that about one-third of the men had gone off to look for food. Even when their officers tried to get them to come back 'they would by no persuasion be induced to return again, giving for answer that they were starving, and said to their officers that they might shoot them if they pleased, but they could not go back till they got meat'.

In spite of this, the Prince ordered the march to begin, and Lord George Murray set off with about 2,000 men, followed by Lord John Drummond with another group, and then the Prince with the French troops; but they had gone only a short distance when messages began to come up from the rear asking those in front to go more slowly. Even though they had guides who knew the country, the way was very rough and often marshy, the men could not be kept together, and many began to fall out of the lines due to weakness from lack of food. Lord George soon saw that he would not have enough troops to carry out his share of the plan; and, since there was now a half-mile gap between the front and rear columns of the Prince's army, it was also obvious that they would be too late to make the attack by the time the others caught up. Most of the other officers agreed with this decision, for dawn was near and a drum had been heard in Cumberland's camp, which showed that they were on the alert, so orders were given to turn back.

Charles was furious, for he did not understand the situation and had not been at the front of the column to see what was happening. 'What can be the matter? What does this mean?' he asked when he found that the retreat had begun. 'We were equal in numbers and could have blown them to the devil.' When he was finally convinced that it was hopeless to go on, the Prince encouraged the men by saying 'There's no help for it, my lads, march back. We shall meet them later and behave like brave fellows.' But ever afterwards he had great doubts about Lord George's faithfulness, and even, it is said, had him watched in case he tried to betray him.

The Battle

The army got back to Culloden about 6 a.m. on Wednesday,
16 April, and Lord Elcho, one of the Prince's officers, tells us

Lord Elcho

that:

> 'Everybody seemed to think of nothing but Sleep. The
> men were prodigiously tired with hunger and fatigue, and
> vast numbers of them went into Inverness, and the Villages
> about, both to Sleep and to pick up what little nourish-
> ment they Could gett. The principal officers went all to the
> house of Culloden and were so much tired that they never
> thought of Calling a Council what was to be done, but
> Every one lay'd himself down where he Could.'

Another writer says that, though orders had been given for
bringing up food and drink for the men:

> 'Through their great want of sleep, meat and drink, many
> slipt off to take some refreshment in Inverness, Culloden,

and the neighbourhood, and others to three or four miles distance, where they had friends and acquaintances; and the said refreshment so lulled them asleep, that designing only to take ane hours rest or two they were afterwards surprised and killed in their beds. By this means we wanted in the action at least one third of our best men.'

As we have seen, many of the officers were alarmed because the choice of battlefield was not a good one, and several had tried to make the Prince agree to a retreat into more hilly ground which would give the Highlanders an advantage, but Charles refused all these appeals, and, by doing so, he ensured his own defeat. If the Jacobite army had fallen back to Inverness they would have been able to get a good supply of food, they could have got in all the stragglers from their army, and they would have been joined by the reinforcements which were already on their way, as well as having a better battle ground; but the commander of the Irish troops settled matters by saying sneeringly that 'The Scots are always good troops till things come to a crisis.' The Highland chiefs were so angry at this undeserved remark that they were ready to fight anywhere at all in order to prove it to be untrue.

About two hours after their return to Culloden news was brought that the Duke's army had been spotted only four miles away, for Cumberland had heard of the failure of the night march, and had wisely decided not to allow the Prince's army time to rest. Officers now hurried round to get their men together and march them to the chosen battlefield, and the Prince went down with the first of them, speaking encouragingly to the men as a good commander should. 'Here they are coming, my lads, we'll soon be with them. They don't forget Gladsmuir [Prestonpans] nor Falkirk, and you have the same arms and swords. Let me see yours,' he said to one of the men. 'I'll answer this will cut off some heads and arms today. Go on, my lads, the day will be ours and we'll want for nothing after.'

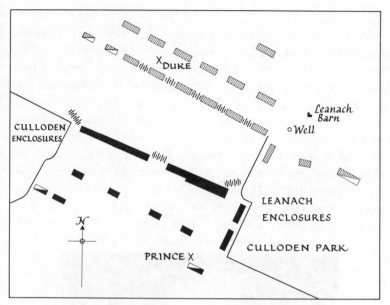

Plan of the battle of Culloden

If you look at the plan on this page you will see how the two armies were drawn up. The Jacobites had about 5,000 men in two lines with a small reserve behind, and the right wing was commanded by Lord George Murray, the centre by Lord John Drummond and the left by the Duke of Perth. The left wing was partly made up of MacDonald regiments, and before the battle it is said that they claimed that they should have the post of honour on the right of the line, and that they were very annoyed when this was refused. The Prince had only twelve guns of different *calibres*, which made the problem of ammunition supply very difficult, and there were only a few trained gunners. These guns were placed in the centre and at the right and left of the front line, in groups of four. The Jacobites were also very short of cavalry. What they had was placed behind the second line, but there was not enough to make any difference to the battle or to protect the retreat after it, though those that were there did their best.

When he was about two miles away from the Prince's position, the Duke of Cumberland formed his army into line of battle, and, soon after 1 p.m. the two forces were within a few hundred yards of each other. As you can see from the plan, the Jacobite army was at first drawn up between two walls which were only 700 yards apart, and, as this did not give them enough room when all the men had arrived, Lord George Murray moved the Atholl Brigade forward and to the left, so that they would be able to charge straight at the enemy; and then formed the right wing into six lines instead of three to prevent overcrowding. This movement made the front line askew, and, since the Prince's best chance of victory was an attack by the whole front line at once, the Duke of Perth was

The Duke of Perth

told to bring up the left wing; but, perhaps because they were still angry because they had been refused the position on the right of the line, the MacDonalds would not move forward.

Before the battle begins, let us look for a moment at the men who made up the Prince's army. Perhaps, after reading about some of their exploits, you may imagine that they were all big, strong men and very fierce fighters; but, we have already seen that this was not the case, and, though we do know that there were some very big men in the army, the average height may have been about 5 feet 4 inches. Of course, most of the men must have been very fit and well able to withstand all kinds of hardships, but it is also surprising to know that there were quite a few who were fifty years of age and over (fifty was then considered to be quite old), and a good number of young boys too. An English spy tells us 'There are a great number of them perfect herd-boys, without arms, stockings or shoes, about 14 to 16 years of age.' The older men and the boys would probably be placed in the rear ranks and the stronger men and better fighters in the front; and, had we been able to walk down the lines before the battle, we would have seen not only the chiefs at the head of their clans, the commanding officers conferring together, the messengers galloping from one point to another, but also the many ordinary people who made up the rank and file of the Jacobite forces. There were farmers and crofters, of course, and tradesmen of all kinds: there were brewers, butchers, bakers, sailors, fishermen, tailors, weavers, herdsmen, ploughmen and blacksmiths, as well as men who followed more uncommon occupations, like James Bradshaw of Manchester, who was a *chapman*; William Leith from Aberdeen, who was a snuff-grinder; Alexander Smith, who belonged to the county of Angus, and who made wigs; James Ogilvy, a tinker, who came from Barry in Forfar; and a sail-weaver called John Russell, who may have been a friend of his, for he came from the same place. But no matter

Orders at Culloden from the 14th to the 15th 1746

Parol   Rice Hemigh (King James)

It is His Royal Highness's positive orders that every person attach himself to some corps of the army, & remain with that corps night and day untile the Battle and pursute be finaly over, this regards the foot as well as the Horse. The Order of Battle is to be given to every Generall officer and every Commander of a Regiement or squadron. It is required & expected of each individual in the army as well officer as Souldier that he keep the post that shall be aloted him, and if any man turn his back to run away, the next behind such man is to shoot him. No body upon pain of Death to strip slain or plunder till the Battle be over. The Highlanders to be in their Kilts and no body to throw away their guns.

By His Royal Highness Command George Murray
Leutenant Generall of His
Majesties Forces

Lord George's orders for the battle

who they were, from the great clan chiefs down to the servants in charge of the baggage, all were tired out and hungry as they stood in their ranks, with a cold wind driving heavy sleet showers in their faces, and listened to the kettledrums of the regular troops advancing towards them across Culloden Moor.

Cumberland's men were tired too, for they had marched nearly ten miles that day, but at least they had had their rations of biscuits and cheese and a tot of brandy for breakfast, while the Jacobite soldiers had been lucky if they even got one biscuit. The Duke's 9,000 men were divided into fifteen infantry regiments, which were at first drawn up in three lines of six, six and three regiments; but soon Cumberland moved

View of the battlefield

up two regiments of the third line to add to the right of the first
and second, and moved up one regiment from the second line
and set it at right-angles to the one on the extreme left, as you
can see on the plan. Can you think why this was an important
move? His cavalry was placed on both wings, his ten 3-
pounder guns were in pairs between each regiment of the first
line, and, as well as these, he had two batteries of three mortars
each between the first and second lines. His men were eager to
fight, for some of them had an earlier defeat to avenge and the
march north had been a tiring one with poor billets, though
the fleet of food ships had kept them well supplied with all they
needed. They had also learned a new drill, which they hoped
would help them to withstand the Highland charge. Instead of
each man attacking with his bayonet the man directly in front
of him, he was to attack the man on his right, who, it was
hoped, would have his sword arm raised, and would therefore
be easy to deal with, as he would have his target on his left
arm.

The battle was begun by the artillery battery in the centre

of the Jacobite line, which opened fire in the hope of hitting the Duke, whose position was between the first and second lines, and his guns replied soon after, two of them shooting at the Prince's position behind his second line, so that he was

The Prince

forced to move off to the right. This was a very bad position for a commander, as he could not really see what was happening, and did not realise that Cumberland's artillery was killing and wounding many of his best front-line troops, or that his own artillery was doing very little damage. He hoped that the Duke would soon order an attack, but of course he had no intention of doing this, as he could see that he was winning the battle with his guns alone. This cannonade may have lasted for as much as twenty or twenty-five minutes, and, when the gunners changed over to *grape-shot*, even bigger gaps were torn in the ranks of the clan regiments. As you can guess, it is very difficult to get untrained troops to stand firm and allow themselves to be shot at, and Charles's men were becoming more and more restive and angry, and were demanding to be led against the enemy.

The regiments in the centre were specially eager to attack, and a message was sent to the Prince asking his permission to do so. Charles agreed, but, almost before the message reached the commanders, the whole centre of the Jacobite army rushed forward, led by the fair-haired Colonel Alasdair MacGillivray of Dunmaglas, followed closely by the right wing, led by Lord George Murray. Here is one account of what followed, written by Lord Elcho:

'The Centre joined the right, and in a Sort of mob, without any order or distinction of Corps, mixt together, rush'd in and attack'd the Dukes left wing, and broke the regiments opposite to them in the first line, but the Second line marching up beat them off, and oblidged them to turn their backs, and run away.'

Another description gives us a picture of what the charge looked like from the Duke's army:

'Their spirited advance lasted but a short time and they shifted away to our left. They came up very boldly and fast in a cloud together, sword in hand. They fired their pieces and flung them away. . . . We kept a continued close fire upon them with our small arms; besides two or three of our cannon gave them a close fire with grape-shot, which galled them very much.'

The attack of the Highlanders

As you can see from this description, the charging Highlanders swung to their right as they approached the government army, which may have been due to the heavy fire that
they faced or to an attempt to get round a piece of marshy
ground. As a result, the right wing was crowded against the
Leanach dyke, which you can see in the plan, and so only a
few men were able to use their muskets in case they hit their
friends. Worse still, as they came near the front line, the regiment that the Duke had placed at right-angles to the others
was able to pour in a very deadly fire as the Highlanders
approached, causing many casualties. In spite of all this, the
weight and speed of the attack broke the two regiments in
front of it, but, as we have seen, troops from the second line
came up and 'gave a terrible fire that brought a great many of
them to the ground'. This fire halted the charging men completely, though it is said that Major John MacGillivray, after
killing at least twelve men with his sword, penetrated the
second line before he was brought down himself. The Stewarts,
who had helped to break through the first line, lost ninety-two
men fighting round their banner, which was rescued at last
and carried off wrapped round the body of a man called

Donald Livingstone. The Clan Chattan banner was rescued in the same way by Donald Mackintosh, who ever afterwards was known as Domhnull na Brataich or Donald of the Flag. A nineteenth-century historian describes the fight between the lines in this way:

'Maddened by despair, and utterly regardless of their lives, they rushed on the enemy whom they felt but could not see, amid the cloud of smoke in which their assailants were buried. . . . All that courage, all that despair could do, was done. . . . Almost every man in their front ranks, Chief and gentleman, fell before the deadly weapons which they braved.'

At last, those few Highlanders who were still alive, most of them wounded, all exhausted, some of them even without their targets and with broken swords, retreated as best they could through the storm of fire which the government troops sent after them.

Meanwhile, what had happened on the other side of the line? You remember that the MacDonalds on the left wing had refused to advance in order to straighten the line before the battle, and some history books say that they also refused to charge during the battle. While it is true to say that they did not rush forward like the centre and the right, we must remember that many of the men had joined the army only the night before, after long marches; that they were losing men heavily from cannon and musketry fire; and that some of them were almost up to the knees in water, as the ground between them and the Duke's forces was very marshy. In spite of this, they did advance three times quite close to the enemy, and Lord John Drummond walked up and down between the lines to try to get the royal army to fire first. (Try to find out why this was important in a battle in these days.) But the real trouble was that by this time some of the regiments on their right had seen that the battle was lost and had begun to retreat, and the MacDonalds saw that they were in danger of being cut off by the Duke's cavalry, which was then beginning to move forward. Large numbers of them began to follow the other fugitives that had begun to stream away from the battle-field; but not all of them, for Keppoch and his brother Donald refused to do so, and led a charge of some of the other officers and men. Of course, they never had a chance. Keppoch was killed near the centre of the line after being wounded twice not long after his brother had been shot down, Clanranald was severely wounded and many other MacDonalds were killed in this gallant but useless action.

You remember that the Prince had taken up a very poor position at the right of his army and took no real part in directing what went on. One of his officers said afterwards that he thought the Prince had lost his head, but we have already seen that he had no real training in generalship, and he certainly did not show that he had any skill in this direction during the battle. Actually it is quite difficult to decide what happened to him as the fighting drew to a close, for there are several different accounts. For example, Lord Elcho, who did not like him, says, 'The Prince . . . turn'd about his horse and went off as soon as the left wing gave way, and never offer'd to rally any of the broken Corps. . . .'; but a Presbyterian minister has written:

'The Prince was in the heat of the action [and] had one of his grooms killed close by him! Major Kennedy, after the Highlanders were broke, went to the Prince and begged he would retire. In this request he was joined by others. The Prince complied with great reluctance, retired in good order and in no hurry.'

(Can you think of at least one reason why there are two such different stories?) It seems likely that Charles may have tried to rally some of the retreating men, but that the defeat of his army was such a shock that one of his officers had to lead his horse from the field.

Lord George Murray, with his usual courage, had led the right wing in the charge and, during the fighting, he had lost one sword and broken another, lost his hat and wig, had several thrusts from bayonets through his coat and been thrown from his horse. Covered in blood and dirt he had rushed back to bring up reinforcements, but it was too late, and all he could do was to organise the retreat of the right wing, which he did with his usual skill. They marched away with colours flying and to the sound of the pipes, but the unfortunate left wing was pursued along the Inverness road by Cumberland's cavalry, and we shall see what happened to them in the next section.

So ended the battle of Culloden, the last chance of the Stuarts to regain the throne of Britain.

The 'Butcher' and the End of the Rebellion

After the actual fighting was over, part of Cumberland's cavalry was ordered to pursue the retreating Highlanders, and part remained on the battlefield. The defeated Jacobite left

The pursuit of the Highland army

D

wing had gone up the Inverness road, and a biography of the Duke says:

'They were pursued by Kingston's Light Horse, and mangled terribly, while the Soldiers, warm in their Resentment, stabbed some of the wounded. . . . The Troops were enraged at their Hardships and Fatigues during a Winter campaign; the habit of the enemy was strange, their Language was still stranger, and their mode of Fighting unusual; the Fields of Preston and Falkirk were still fresh in their Memories.'

Not only were many Jacobite soldiers killed by these horsemen, but also people who had no connection with the battle at all, such as two old weavers at a little village and a man and his nine-year-old son who had been ploughing in a field nearby. Even worse than this was the way the wounded were treated on the battlefield, where the Hanoverian troops

WELL OF THE DEAD HERE THE CHIEF OF THE MACGILLIVRAYS FELL

The Well of the Dead

went about killing all who showed any signs of life. As Lord Elcho said, 'Everybody that fell into their hands got no quarters'; another eye-witness wrote that, 'our men, what with killing the enemy, dabbling their feet in the blood and splashing it about one another, looked like so many butchers.' After reading that, it is not surprising to find that three of the troopers specially congratulated by Cumberland for their work in the pursuit actually were butchers from Nottingham. The Duke himself gave his men an example of what he wanted done by ordering the wounded Colonel Fraser of Inverallochy to be shot when he admitted that he was one of the Prince's followers.

No attempt was made to give the wounded any medical attention, and those who were not killed on the spot were stripped of their clothes and possessions and left to die. The excuse given for this brutality was that an order had been

The graves of the clans

issued to the Jacobite soldiers to give no quarter if they won, but this has since been proved to be a forgery added to a captured Jacobite order. For the next two days the search for fugitives went on. Twelve wounded men were removed from a house on the excuse that they were to be seen by a surgeon, and were shot down outside. Eighteen officers were shot at Culloden House; and about thirty men were found in a barn near the battlefield, which was then tightly fastened and set on fire, not one of the men escaping. No one knows how many

The cairn commemorating the battle

wounded men were murdered in this way, but it has been calculated that at least 180 men were found, taken back to the battlefield and shot there.

It is likely that the Prince's army lost between 1,000 and 1,200 men in the battle, and many more were taken prisoner. There are records of 3,471 prisoners all told, but, of course, many of these had not been at the battle, but had been arrested because they had sympathised with the Jacobites or had helped them in some way. The treatment of these prisoners was also very cruel. Here is an account written by a medical officer who visited one of the ships on which the men were imprisoned:

'I went on board the vessel called the "Pamela", . . . and, on my looking down into the hold where the prisoners then were, was saluted with such an intolerable smell that it was like to overcome me, tho' I was provided with proper herbs and my nostrils stuffed therewith. . . . the prisoners were called up one by one, such as were able to come. . . . The number of those who came on deck were fifty-four, many of whom were very ill as appeared by their countenance and their snail creep pace in ascending the ladder, being only just able to crawl up. . . .

To hear the description given by the Guard who went into the Hold of the uncleanliness of that place is surpassing imagination, and too nautious to describe.'

Here is another description, written by a prisoner after the capture of Carlisle:

'We were barbarously treated, the souldiers rifling us and taking everything of value from us, both money and Cloaths; they did not offer us any Provisions for three days, and on the fourth but one small Bisket a man. They broke open a well which had not been used for upwards of an hundred years.

'We was oblig'd to drink that or die of thirst. . . . our Jaylour thought it proper to keep our pay and provide us with victuals, which were but very indifferent, consisting of cows heads, livers, lights, and the refuse of the market, which threw most of us into the Flux.'

At last it was decided that the trials of the prisoners should be in England, as the government did not think that a jury of Scotsmen would find many of them guilty; but, since there were so many of them, it was decided to 'lot' the prisoners—that is, select one man in every twenty for trial. Of course,

The execution of Lord Balmerino and Lord Kilmarnock

Lord Lovat

those leaders who had been captured were not included in this, and Lord Balmerino, Lord Kilmarnock and Lord Lovat were all executed, though Lord Lovat had not really been 'out' in the rebellion, due to his age; 120 others were hanged, 936 were transported, 222 were banished and 58 escaped. The lists show that 88 died in prison, but they also show 684 prisoners whose fate is not known, and it is more than likely that many of these died in prison also. Finally, 1,287 were either exchanged or released as prisoners of war and 76 got a conditional pardon.

Of course, this was not all. The government also passed laws to make sure that another rebellion would never again take place. They took away the old powers of the chiefs, so that they could not force their clansmen to follow them in another rising. They also passed a very strict Disarming Act, with six months' imprisonment for the first offence and seven years' transporta-

Loch nan Uamh, where the Prince embarked for France

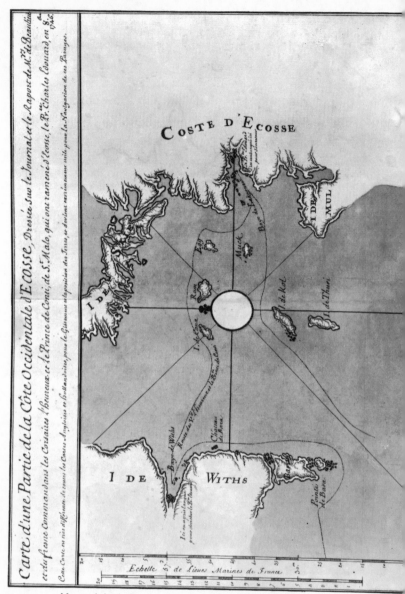

Carte d'une Partie de la Côte Occidentale d'Ecosse, Dressée sur le Journal et le Raport de M.rs de Beaulieu et autres Commandans les Corsaires l'heureux et le Prince de Conti, de S.t Malo, qui ont ramené d'Ecosse, le P.ce Charles Edouard, en 8.bre 1746.

Cette Carte en très différente de toutes les Cartes Angloises et Hollandoises, pour le Gisement et la position des Terres, et doivent extrémement aider pour la Navigation de ces Parages.

COSTE D'ECOSSE

I DE MUL

I DE WITHS

Echelle de Lieues Marines de France

Map made by the French commanders of the ships which came for the Prince

96

tion for the second; and this Act also forbade the playing of the bagpipes and the wearing of the tartan. Finally, the Episcopalian Church, which had always supported the Prince, was punished in a number of ways.

And what of the Prince himself? As you all know, he wandered through the Highlands for more than five months after Culloden, but, in spite of the reward of £30,000 for his capture, he was never betrayed, though many people knew where he was, and many, including the famous Miss Flora MacDonald, helped him to avoid his pursuers. The story of

Miss Flora MacDonald

his adventures would almost fill another book, and if you look at the section called Things To Do, you can see there some suggestions which will help you to learn more about the later life of the man who is still remembered as Bonnie Prince Charlie.

HOW DO WE KNOW?

So many books have been written about the 1745 Rising that it would be impossible to put them all down here, and you would certainly not have time to read them all and do your other work in school as well! Thus, only those books which you are likely to find most useful and which will help you to do some of the exercises are included in this section. The books marked like this * will help you with the exercises based on the map on page 100.

This section is divided into three parts. The first lists a number of books which were written about the time of the Rising: the second gives a list of some of the histories which were written some time afterwards, some of them in this century—we call this 'secondary material': and the third part mentions some books of fiction. If you are reading any of the books mentioned in the first part, you must be careful to try to find out which side the writer supported, otherwise you will get a one-sided picture of the Rising. Even in the second part, you will see that three books definitely favour the Jacobite side; but, as you know, a real historian does not favour one side or the other, and you must try to be quite impartial when working through the exercises in 'Things To Do'.

First of all, here are some of the books from which we get the source material that helps us to write history—that is, books, diaries and memoirs which were written by people who lived at the time, or were eye-witnesses of some of the things that happened. The first two were written by men who were both officers in the Prince's army; *A Short Account of the Affairs of Scotland in the Years 1744, 1745, 1746* (Edinburgh, Douglas), by Lord Elcho; and *Memoirs of the Rebellion in Scotland in 1745 and 1746* by the Chevalier Johnstone (Folio Society, 1958). You might find it interesting to compare these accounts with *A Compleat History of the Rebellion*, written by a volunteer in the Duke of Cumberland's army called James Ray, or to compare Ray's book with *A History of the Rebellion in the Year 1745*, by John Home, who was taken prisoner at Falkirk. The next two books were both written by the same man, Andrew Henderson, and they are called *The History of the Rebellion, 1745 and 1746*, and *The Life of William Augustus, Duke of Cumberland*. Finally, here are two collections of accounts written at the time of the Rising. The first is *The Lyon in Mourning** (Scottish History Society), and is made up of a number of journals and narratives of people who took part in the '45, collected by Robert Forbes, who was the Bishop of Ross and Caithness: and the other is *The Rising of 1745** by C. S. Terry (Cambridge University Press), a book of extracts from writings made at the time.

You would find a great deal of information about the Prince's movements from the *Itinerary of Prince Charles Edward Stuart*, compiled by W. B. Blaikie (Scottish History Society), but you would have to borrow this book from a big library. Other books which you would find useful, but which were not written at the time, are *The Prince in the Heather* by Eric Linklater (Hodder and Stoughton); *Prince Charles Edward and the '45** (Hale); *In the Steps of Bonnie Prince Charlie** (Rich), both by Winifred Duke; *The Jacobite General* by K. Tomasson (Blackwood) and *Battles of the '45* by K. Tomasson and F. Buist (Batsford); *Culloden* by John Prebble (Secker and Warburg), and *Culloden*, the guidebook written for the National Trust for Scotland by Colonel Cameron Taylor; *The Life and Adventures of Prince Charles Edward Stuart* by W. B. Norrie; *1715* (Nelson) and *1745 and After* (Nelson), both by A. and H. Taylor; and *The Jacobite Movement; the Last Phase*, by Sir Charles Petrie (Eyre and Spottiswoode), though we must remember that the writers of the last three books favoured the Jacobite side. Finally, you would find that *The Young Adventurer* by D. Nicholas (Batchworth), and *The Quest Forlorn* by C. H. Hartmann (Heinemann), both give fair accounts of the Rising.

Last of all, here are some stories which you might like to read—perhaps some of them are in your school library. *The Bull Calves* by Naomi Mitchison (Cape); *The Flight of the Heron, The Gleam in the North* and *The Dark Mile*, all by D. K. Broster (Heinemann); *The Grey Pilot* by Angus MacVicar (Burke); *The Hunted Head* by Olivia Fitzroy (Cape); and *Lanterns over the Lune* by Kathleen Fidler (Lutterworth).

You are sure to want to learn some Jacobite songs, and you will find that most school song books and collections of Scottish songs have got at least one or two in them; but if you want to try exercise 4 in 'Things To Do Together', you will find twenty-two songs with music in a book called *Prince Charlie and the '45*. These songs have been arranged by Alan Reid and the book is published by Bayley and Ferguson. Another good book is *The Jacobite Relics of Scotland* collected by James Hogg, but not all the songs have music, and you would need to borrow the book from a library. You will also find some songs at the end of *Poems and Ballads of Scottish History*, edited by Dewar M. Robb (Blackie); and there are some little-known songs on the Topic record 12T79, called *The Jacobite Rebellions*. The songs are sung by Ewan McColl, and there is some interesting information about them on the cover of the record.

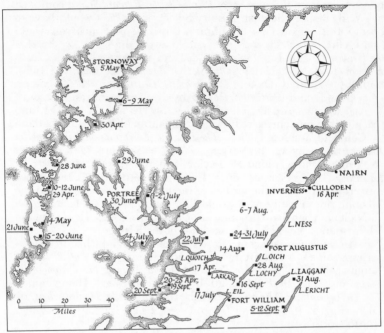

Map of the Prince's wanderings in the Highlands

On the map on this page showing Prince Charlie's Wanderings, you will see a number of big dots, with a date or dates beside each one. Each dot marks a place where the Prince stayed or where he hid from the troops that were pursuing him.

In order to do the exercises below, you will need a very good atlas or a big map of the area, and also some of the books which are marked with an asterisk in the section called 'How Do We Know?'

1. Copy or trace the map into your notebook, put in all the dots very carefully, and then join them up with a coloured line in their correct order, starting at 16 April and ending at 20 September. This will show you the route followed by the Prince in his wanderings but, since it is not possible to show all the places that he went to on a map of this size, the route will not be quite accurate.

2. The names of some of the places that he went to have been put on the map to help you. Try to get a large-scale map of the

area so that you can add others for yourself.

3. Seven of the dates have been underlined to show that something of interest or importance happened at these places. You can find out from some of the books in the 'How Do We Know?' section what these events were. Try to describe each one in your own words, or draw a picture of what you think might have happened.

4. Using the information which you have found out in the previous exercises, describe the Prince's wanderings as they might have been written up by the special correspondent of a newspaper, illustrating your article with little drawings; OR, write the script for a television programme entitled 'Pursuit of a Prince'. Bring in as many real characters as you can, and use one of the Prince's companions as narrator.

5. Collect as many pictures as you can of the places where the Prince stayed while waiting to get a ship to France, and on separate sheets of paper write descriptions of anything important that happened there, where the Prince had come from and where he went to afterwards, and then stick both pictures and descriptions on the back of a roll of wallpaper as a frieze for your classroom.

6. Try to find out all you can about the Loch Arkaig treasure, and write a little note about it in your jotters.

7. Draw a map of the roads constructed by General Wade after the Rising of 1715.

8. Draw a picture of the fight between the 'Elizabeth' and the 'Lion'.

9. Compose a proclamation offering a reward for the capture of the Prince.

10. Draw a picture of the Prince in the cottage on the island of Eriskay.

11. Write an eye-witness account of the raising of the standard at Glenfinnan; or draw the scene as you imagine it may have appeared to the Prince's supporters.

12. Compose the kind of speech that might have been made by the Prince to his men at Glenfinnan.

13. Draw a picture of the Jacobite army entering Edinburgh.

14. Learn the words and tune of the song 'Hey, Johnny Cope'.

15. Write a newspaper account of the Jacobite march into England, adding suitable headlines.

16. Draw a picture of the Jacobite army climbing Shap as it is described in the book.

17. Find out some of the exciting incidents in the battle of Culloden, and describe them in your own words.

18. Draw a picture of the charge of the Jacobite right wing at Culloden, or the retreat of the left wing.
19. Write obituary notices for any two of the following people: Prince Charlie; Lord George Murray; Cameron of Lochiel; the Duke of Cumberland; Duncan Forbes of Culloden; Sir John Cope; General Wade.
20. Describe any incidents in the Rising which may have occurred either in your home district or near it.
21. Try to find out what the most important results of the Rising were for the Highlands and for Scotland, and write a short note about them.
22. Make a list of all the Jacobite songs that you know or can find out about, arranging them in two columns in your notebook, one containing those songs written about the time of the Rising and one of songs written afterwards. Write a note about them, saying which ones you like, and why. Ask your music teacher to help you to learn one of each kind.
23. Try to find out what two well-known pieces of music are connected in some way with the Duke of Cumberland; and also the words of the fourth verse of 'God Save The King'.

THINGS TO DO TOGETHER

1. Compose a dialogue between the Prince and Cameron of Locheil which might have been spoken before Cameron decided to join the Prince, and act it in front of the class.
2. Write an imaginary scene between the Provost and bailies of Glasgow and Prince Charlie's officers when the latter demanded clothing for the Jacobite army.
3. Write a short play based on the scene when the chiefs decided that it was necessary to turn back at Derby. Think of all the possible arguments that could be used by the Prince for going on and by the chiefs for going back.
4. Make a list of all the songs that you think describe best the important events in the Rising, then get the class to divide into groups which will learn one or two of these songs each. With the help of a narrator to link up the songs with short descriptions of the events that they described, the whole class can then produce a picture of the Rising in music. Ask your teacher to put the whole programme on the tape-recorder, so that it can be used later.

GLOSSARY

Adjutant, an officer whose duty it is to assist the commanding officer

aide-de-camp, an officer who carries the general's orders and who assists him in various ways

arbitrary, absolute

barck, a three-masted sailing vessel

baubles, worthless ornaments

branders, a frame of metal bars used in cooking

calibre, the diameter of the bore of a gun

chapman, a pedlar

chase=chaise, a light carriage for one or more people

Chevalier, a knight

claymores, large swords used by the Highlanders

commission of regency, a document giving Charles the powers of a regent

constrent, hindrance

Covenanters, supporters of the National Covenant of 1638 or the Solemn League and Covenant of 1643

deduced, pointed out

dismounted, thrown off their carriages

to double, to pass round

dragoons, cavalry

durst, dared

Elector, the title of certain princes and archbishops who had the right to elect the Holy Roman Emperor

engage in the attempt, take part in the rising

entertain no notion, not consider the idea

field pieces, cannons used on the actual battle field

flints, small pieces of hard stone used in firing muskets

gate-porter, a gate keeper

gazettes, newspapers

girt, fastened

goes ill, does not progress

grape-shot, shot which scatters when it is fired

heir-apparent, the person recognized as the next ruler after the death of the king or queen

Heralds, officers who made proclamations, arranged ceremonies and kept a record of coats of arms

high treason, an attempt to overthrow the government

Holy Roman Emperor, the name given to the ruler of the German Empire until the nineteenth century

illuminate, to light up or ornament windows in honour of some person or event *imperious*, commanding

intelligence, information

Jacobite, follower of James *(Jacobus)*

languish, lose strength

lay, remained

levée, a morning assembly held by a ruler or an important person

to levy, to raise

Lord President of the Court of Session, the head of the first division of the highest civil court in Scotland

madder, a plant whose root could be used to make a red dye

making terms, surrendering on the promise of pardon

manifest, the public declaration of what the leader of a party intends to do

mortars, guns which fire their shells high in the air so that they drop right on the enemy's position

Nonconformists, people other than Roman Catholics who do not belong to the Anglican Church

outflanked, the wing of one army being extended beyond the wing of the opposing army

owing allegiance, owing loyalty to a noble or chief

pawn, to give something in security for the repayment of money that has been borrowed

persuaded, certain

plantations, English colonies in what is now the United States of America

played, fired

port, the gate of a town

Portmantle, a bag for carrying clothing

Pursuivants, attendants on a Herald

Quarter-master General, an officer who looks after billets and supplies for soldiers

to reconnoitre, to look at or survey

robust, strong

to sack, to plunder

stature, height

succours, aid

targets, small shields

total decay, complete poverty

train bands, bands of citizens trained as soldiers

twin, come out

verdigris, a green substance got from copper and used as a medicine or dye

Walloons, natives of part of Belgium

well-affected, inclined to support